"In her delightful style, Lois Tverberg engagingly leads us across cultures to begin to envision a different worldview, a worldview more consistent with the world of most of Scripture. In so doing, she brings alive biblical texts from the inside."

Craig S. Keener, F. M. and Ada Thompson Professor of Biblical Studies, Asbury Theological Seminary

"Thanks to the good work of biblical scholars, the historical Jesus of Nazareth is once again situated in his divinely designed Second Temple period Jewish context. The next critical step is to understand that hearing him in his original setting equips us to follow him more faithfully in ours. The latest from Lois Tverberg is a meaningful contribution to that end. Read this book for a more informed reading of The Book."

James C. Whitman, president, Center for Judaic-Christian Studies

"In *Reading the Bible with Rabbi Jesus*, Lois Tverberg opens up the Scriptures we all love and shines a fascinating new light on them. As she gracefully bridges the culture gap between Jesus' first Jewish followers and twenty-first century Christians and unites the Old and New Testaments, I found myself falling in love with the Bible all over again. Lois is a superb teacher, using story and gentle humor to great effect. I devoured this fascinating book. Highly recommended!"

Lynn Austin, author of *Where We Belong*

"Just what exactly did Jesus share with his disciples on the road to Emmaus? This excellent book unfolds so many valuable truths in the Scriptures that are often ignored or misunderstood. Lois Tverberg is a trustworthy guide whose insightful discoveries provide a delightful appetizer to some of the most exciting passages in the Old Testament. I'm recommending it to everyone I know."

Todd Bolen, professor of biblical studies, The Master's University

"Lois Tverberg is back with her most insightful work yet. Every chapter takes us on a journey of discovery, opening our eyes to astounding realities and clarifying confusing or misunderstood passages that have significant impact in our reading of the Bible and our relationship with Jesus Christ. Every Christian should read this book!"

Brad Gray, author of *Make Your Mark* and founder of *Walking The Text Ministries*

"Though the truth in the written Word of God transcends time, place, and culture, understanding the Bible's context adds depth of meaning to every jot and tittle it contains. Lois Tverberg is an apt guide to the Jewish context of the Bible, and her mix of thoughtful research and relatable application will help readers discover new riches within its pages. She offers an entry ramp to the time, place, and culture in which the Bible was first given with the goal of enriching not only personal reading and study but also strengthening the church in her identity and mission here and now. Highly recommended!"

Michelle Van Loon, author of *Moments & Days: How Our Holy Celebrations Shape Our Faith*

"In *Reading the Bible with Rabbi Jesus*, Lois Tverberg gives us a front row seat at the feet of Jesus as familiar passages in the Bible come alive. By taking us on a journey into the culture of the first century and the Hebraic mindset of Jesus, Lois teaches us how to bend our ear to hear the Galilean accent of our Jewish Rabbi. Open your Bible, grab a highlighter, and dive into the world of the first century like never before."

Robby Gallaty, pastor of Long Hollow Baptist Church and author of *The Forgotten Jesus*

"Lois Tverberg has written still another classic *Reading the Bible with Rabbi Jesus* compliments her *Walking in the Dust of Rabbi Jesus*, but goes beyond. Tverberg clarifies what it meant to study 'Moses and all the Prophets' with the sage from Galilee, Yeshua of Nazareth. For those who want to know what it was like to be one of Jesus' inner circle of disciples and sit down with him to study Scripture, Tverberg's new book is the place to start."

David N. Bivin, founder and editor of *Jerusalem Perspective*

"How odd of God / To choose the Jews." It is not certain who wrote that epigram and why, but what is certain is that God did indeed choose the Jews to show us what he is like. His Son *Yeshua*, whom we know as Jesus, was a Jew. How wonderfully and mysteriously strange is the incarnation! That the infinite maker of heaven and earth would definitively reveal himself in a particular man, of a particular ethnicity, in a particular culture, who spoke a particular language, in a particular time and place in history. Lois Tverberg's splendid book explores that divine oddity with clarity, good humor, and even startling insight, showing how Jesus the first century Jew is oddly the Savior and Lord of all peoples in all times and places."

Ben Patterson, campus pastor, Westmont College

READING *THE* BIBLE *WITH* RABBI JESUS

How a Jewish Perspective Can Transform Your Understanding

LOIS TVERBERG

BakerBooks
a division of Baker Publishing Group
Grand Rapids, Michigan

Published by Baker Books
a division of Baker Publishing Group
PO Box 6287, Grand Rapids, MI 49516-6287
www.bakerbooks.com

Printed in the United States of America

Library of Congress Cataloging-in-Publication Data
Names: Tverberg, Lois, author.
Title: Reading the Bible with Rabbi Jesus : how a Jewish perspective can transform your understanding / Lois Tverberg.
Description: Grand Rapids : Baker Books, 2018. | Includes bibliographical references and index.
Identifiers: LCCN 2017028376 | ISBN 9780801017155 (cloth)
Subjects: LCSH: Bible. Old Testament—Criticism, interpretation, etc., Jewish.
Classification: LCC BS1186 .T84 2018 | DDC 221.6—dc23
LC record available at https://lccn.loc.gov/2017028376

Published in association with the literary agency of Ann Spangler and Company, Grand Rapids, Michigan.

18 19 20 21 22 23 7 6 5 4 3 2

In loving memory of my mother,
Laura Evelyn Ritland Tverberg
1922–2017

Charm is deceptive, and beauty is fleeting;
but a woman who fears the LORD is to be praised.
Honor her for all that her hands have done,
and let her works bring her praise at the city gate.

Proverbs 31:30–31 NIV

Contents

1

✳ ✳ ✳

Opening the Bible with Jesus

Emmaus Is Still There

Have you ever tasted fresh pita bread made by the Bedouins? It's out of this world—chewy and hot, crispy in spots, and a little smoky from the open fire. When a veiled, wizened old woman flops a piping-hot piece into your hands, you need to tear a chunk off and pass the rest on before your fingers burn. Smeared with olive oil and dried hyssop, it's like nothing you've ever tasted before.

Sure, you can buy bagged pita bread in your local grocery store, and its nutritional value will be exactly the same. But the mouthwatering aroma of the original simply can't be captured and transported to you. Similarly, the Bible's ideas are often best appreciated "freshly served" in their original Middle Eastern setting.

This is what this book, *Reading the Bible with Rabbi Jesus*, is all about—helping you mentally transport yourself back in place and time to read the Bible afresh, as one of Jesus' first-century disciples.

Maybe you've noticed the latest food trend: everyone seems to be into "artisanal" foods. They want to savor authentic flavors, taste food from centuries-old recipes. They love organic cheeses and heirloom vegetables, farmers' markets and food co-ops. People want to eat *slow* food, not fast food. It takes more time and effort, but it's worth it, they say.

You know what? I'm into artisanal Bible study.

A lot of us do Bible study microwave-style. We gulp down a prepackaged, presweetened devotion with a few slurps of coffee before heading off to work. Is it at all surprising when it's bland and unmemorable, like a vending-machine sandwich?

You know how at the end of every cooking show the hosts dish up for themselves a plateful of whatever they've been making? Their lip-smacking pleasure over each mouthwatering morsel makes you want to reach right through the screen and take a bite yourself. This is my world, and I invite you to join me. I don't think a day has gone by that some insight from the biblical world hasn't made my reading more flavorful.

Studying this way takes more time, of course. Not everyone has time to learn ancient languages, historical details, and cultural ideas, but you'll be surprised how every little bit of learning is helpful. It's the same as with cooking. Not everyone can raise their own vegetables and cook from scratch, but adding even a few fresh herbs and local ingredients can liven up any meal.

My personal specialty is serving up the Scriptures Mediterranean-style. Twenty years ago I was turned on to the importance of studying the Bible in its original Eastern, Jewish context, and I've been looking at Christ through that lens ever since.

I've written two books about Rabbi Jesus before now. In *Sitting at the Feet of Rabbi Jesus* (Zondervan, 2009), Ann Spangler and I explored Jesus' first-century world of rabbis, disciples, festivals, prayers, and the Torah, and showed how his Jewish setting sheds light on the life and ministry of Christ. Later on, in *Walking in the Dust of Rabbi Jesus* (Zondervan, 2012), I dove deeper into some of Jesus' most important sayings in their Jewish context and considered the implications for us as twenty-first-century disciples.

Now, in *Reading the Bible with Rabbi Jesus*, I want to look at some ways we can mentally bridge the culture gap between his Middle Eastern, Jewish world and ours in order to read the Bible as natives. How can ordinary Christians be equipped to read the Bible from the Hebraic perspective of its first readers? What big-picture ideas do we need to understand? These are questions that I've been asking myself since I started studying the Bible's cultural context.

Embracing Jesus' Jewishness is a fairly recent development in Christian scholarship. In the past few decades, we've been realizing that Jesus has been overly cast within Greco-Roman society to the neglect of his Jewish context. Jesus interacted with a wide spectrum of people—Samaritans, Romans, Greeks—yet his Galilean upbringing and ministry were profoundly, deeply Jewish.[1] While we find Paul preaching to Greek audiences, Jesus' words fit far better into Judaism than a Gentile context. What are the implications? Seeing him in his context sheds brilliant new light on his ministry and deepens our understanding of his words.

A Bible in a Gilded Cage

Truthfully, before I "tasted" the Bible served in its original setting, a lot of it was hard for me to swallow. From my upbringing I was convinced that it was the inspired Word of God, but I found much of it more bewildering than inspiring. The last quarter of my Bible, starting with the book of Matthew, was dog-eared, rippled with coffee mug circles, and filled with highlighting and thoughts penciled into the margins. The first three-fourths, however, remained immaculate.

One of my favorite things about a new Bible is the gilded page edging. As you gently flex the leather covers, the gossamer pages flutter softly past, edges gleaming in the light. Once you start thumbing through it regularly, that glint fades. It's like a new box of crayons. A tiny rainbow army salutes you when you first open the box, the multihued points standing at perfect attention. But to actually color with them, you're forced to mar this pristine beauty. Personally, I used to draw with the bottom ends for a while, just to keep the box nice.

Much of the gilded edging of my Bible used to last a very long time too. This wasn't because I was trying to keep it nice but rather because I found so much of Scripture frustrating and impenetrable. The unbroken golden edging formed a gilded cage that locked away all the strangeness inside.

Many passages were confounding. Sure, there were some beloved characters early on, like Noah and Abraham. Sunday school flannelgraphs and doe-eyed cartoons made them seem soft and approachable. I couldn't wade in much past Exodus, though, before I hit deep water. Soon I would be adrift in a sea of sacrifices and begats and obscure historical details. Nobody would admit it, but the New Testament was tough at times too. Some of Jesus' sayings sounded deliberately obtuse. The kingdom is like a fishing net, a seed, a weedy field . . . what? Not to mention Revelation, with all its beasts and plagues.

I envied no one more than the two disciples who encountered Jesus on the Emmaus road in Luke 24, whose hearts burned as an incognito Christ led them on a backcountry hike through their Bible, when "beginning with Moses and all the Prophets, he interpreted to them in all the Scriptures the things concerning himself" (Luke 24:27).

Wouldn't it have been great to have heard Jesus connect all the dots to show God's great plan all the way through the Bible? If I could get my hands on Marty McFly's DeLorean time machine car, there's no place in history I'd rather go.

Where to Park Your Time Machine

I've already figured out where to park my time machine. A few years ago I spent a winter in a village just northwest of Jerusalem. When I wanted to go into the city I'd take Egged bus #154, which seemed to take forever because we had to pick up passengers from all the nearby villages before entering the city. The massive motor coach seemed ill-suited to the winding lanes. It would lumber back and forth across the Judean hillside, the engine groaning and chugging, gears lugging around each curve. The brakes would screech as it descended a series of switchbacks and squeal to a stop one last time in a hamlet called Motza. Everyone would breathe a sigh of relief when the last commuters boarded, anticipating that soon the on-ramp to Highway 1 would appear. Finally, the bus could accelerate up to a modern road speed and join the traffic zooming along the six-lane superhighway into Jerusalem.

At that very last stop in Motza, when the doors would swing open for passengers to board, before the underpass—that's the moment to get off. Stride across the intersection, walk a few dozen yards into the scrub brush, peer through the dried weeds, and you'll see them: the ancient pavers of the Emmaus road, the stones where Jesus' sandals walked.

Yes, these are the real, actual stones. Unlike many tourist destinations in Israel, the ancient pavers are not marked in any way. There are no lights and bells, no gift shops hawking Magnum bars, Ahava hand cream, and holy tchotchkes. You simply have to know where to look. Believe it or not, you are standing where you'd park your time machine if you wanted to travel back to the scene of Jesus' fateful conversation.

Older Bible commentaries say that the site of Emmaus is unknown. Or they pin the location in one of a couple of other places, including Latrun, where a shrine has been venerated as Emmaus for over fifteen hundred years. No one really believes that it's the place because it's more than eighteen miles away, an impossible hike for the disciples to take twice in one day, first with Jesus, and then back into Jerusalem for their breathless report that same evening (v. 33).

Most scholars are now convinced that the Emmaus Luke refers to lies right here, under the village of Motza, about three and a half miles from Jerusalem. Its ancient name was *Ha-motza*, meaning "the spring," which was translated into Greek as *Em-ma-oos*, or Emmaus. Down through the centuries, locals have even known about the ancient Roman road, which was much more visible even a few decades ago. Not many years ago they were still even following the path left by the remaining stones, which made a convenient trail into the Old City, an easy two-hour walk to the Jaffa Gate.[2] This was the "Highway 1" that the ancient world knew.

As I've studied the Bible in its setting, this discovery is typical of the experiences I've had. For centuries we've had to be satisfied with improbable church traditions, but when we look closer at the historical record, we find insights that affirm biblical accounts. Often I discover that locals have known about them all along. And sometimes the reality of the world of Jesus is visible even today, hiding in plain sight.

A Jewish Book in a Gentile World

In the very next story after his encounter at Emmaus, Jesus made another surprising appearance, this time to the rest of his disciples. Again he guided them on a scenic travelogue through the Scriptures, saying,

> "These are my words that I spoke to you while I was still with you, that everything written about me in the Law of Moses and the Prophets and the Psalms must be fulfilled." Then he opened their minds to understand the Scriptures, and said to them, "Thus it is written, that the Christ should suffer and on the third day rise from the dead, and that repentance and the forgiveness of sins should be proclaimed in his name to all nations, beginning from Jerusalem." (vv. 44–47)

Here Jesus refers to his Bible in a very Jewish way, as the "Law of Moses and the Prophets and the Psalms." Two millennia later, this is still the way Jews speak of their Scriptures, what Christians call the "Old Testament" (according to the Protestant canon).[3] Commonly the name is shortened to

Tanakh, deriving its consonants from the first letter of the three divisions, the *Torah* (law or Pentateuch), the *Neviim* (neh-vee-EEM: prophets and historical books), and the *Ketuvim* (keh-too-VEEM: writings: psalms, proverbs, etc.). (See appendix A for the books as they appear in the Tanakh.)

The more I pondered the scene on the Emmaus road, the more remarkable it seemed. Luke 24:27 says that "Beginning with Moses and all the Prophets, [Jesus] interpreted to them in all the Scriptures the things concerning himself." The very texts that I found most intractable, the laws of Moses and the prophetic books, were the ones he was preaching from. Indeed, his favorite books to quote from were Deuteronomy and Isaiah, and he quoted from them *a lot*.

Traveling across Time and Culture

After leading his disciples through these Jewish Scriptures and revealing how they pointed to his life and atoning death, Jesus commissioned them to proclaim this message to all the nations (Matt. 28:19). The word he used there for "nations" was *goyim*, which carries the sense of "Gentiles," or non-Jews.

The more I've studied, the more I've realized the implications of this fact. The Lutheran upbringing I inherited from my Norwegian-American ancestors was thoroughly Gentile. Because I was unfamiliar with the framework of Jesus' original setting, I struggled to grasp many ideas that first-century listeners found in the Scriptures.

Admittedly the Bible is a foreign land to us. But it's not so surprising, considering what happened only a few weeks after the Emmaus conversation. At Pentecost, God's Spirit poured out on the disciples and turned them into *translators*.

God wasted no time in equipping them to carry their message from one language to the next, one society to the next. The farther they went, the more their audience's cultural background shifted. In order to communicate in ways new listeners would understand, they needed to reframe the good news in terms that made sense to their hearers. It is only logical that after the gospel had gone around the world, we would find ourselves at a distance from its origins.

If we had a time machine, we'd know how to go back in time to Emmaus. Yet there is another journey we need to take, from our Western world to its Middle Eastern setting. New Testament scholar Ken Bailey writes,

> The Bible is an Eastern book. We see it through the colored glasses of Western culture. Much is lost. We miss the subtleties of humor and many of the underlying assumptions. We do not understand the ingrained attitudes that illuminate a story or illustration. . . . What lies between the lines, what is felt and not spoken, is of deepest significance.[4]

Indeed, elsewhere Bailey adds,

> Having struggled for more than a generation with this problem in both the East and the West, it is my perception that for us as Westerners the cultural distance "over" to the Middle East is greater than the distance "back" to the first century. The cultural gulf between the West and the East is deeper and wider than the gulf between the first century (in the Middle East) and the contemporary conservative Middle Eastern village.[5]

What a thought—that as much of a hurdle as it seems to travel back in time to the Emmaus road, the gap between us and the biblical world is actually wider *culturally* than *temporally*.

What if we could take our own Emmaus journey with Rabbi Jesus, but this time to open our eyes to the Bible's grand themes within their Hebraic Jewish context? In my earlier book *Sitting at the Feet of Rabbi Jesus*, I focused specifically on the Jewish religious context of Jesus. Here, my focus is on our cultural differences with the non-Western, Hebraic thought-world that is so pervasive in the Bible, both Old and New Testaments. What wisdom can we learn from their worldview? What might we discover about Christ and his mission that we never knew before? That's what I want to share with you, my readers, in this book.

God often expressed his truth to ancient listeners in ways that shepherds and desert wanderers would understand, in metaphors that escape the modern reader. Sensitizing ourselves to the Bible's age-old imagery will allow us to read it with new eyes. Often this perspective brings into focus the merciful, self-sacrificing Father whom Christ knew and loved rather than the harsh caricature of a God many see there.

We'll listen again with first-century ears to the way Jesus spoke to his contemporaries, making it crystal clear that God's promises were and are met in him. By examining how Jesus fulfilled the prophets' expectations, we'll discover startling truths about Christ's mission and our role as his disciples.

We will be equipped to read Scripture with more insight and inspiration by grasping the perspective of its original audience. We'll take a fresh look at key biblical ideas from an Eastern perspective. We'll go on a journey back in time to help us understand how the Jewish people approached life, enabling us to rediscover wisdom that's been largely forgotten and allowing us to read God's Word with depth and insight for our lives today.

TOOLS AND REFLECTIONS

Reading

1. Read Luke 24:13–35, paying attention to the conversation going on between Jesus and the disciples.

   What phrases do they use that are not clear to you?

   What questions does it raise?

   What ideas are assumed by the readers?

   What do you think Jesus said when he used Scripture to explain his mission?

2. If you traveled to a traditional community in the Middle East today, what cultural differences would you expect to encounter compared with where you live?

3. Take a look at appendix A, which lists the three divisions of books of the Hebrew Bible. Compare it with the table of contents in your own Bible. Are there any books that surprise you by where they are placed?

4. What specifically is of interest to you about the Jewishness of the Bible?

Thoughts for Going Deeper

- If you want to know more about the *real* Emmaus road, search for it on the JerusalemPerspective.com website.

The editor, David Bivin, was the one who first showed me the ancient road. Look for his recent report, which explains that because the pavers are not being actively preserved, they are in danger of being lost. (This online journal also contains a wealth of excellent articles on the first-century Jewish context of Jesus.)

PART 1

Repacking Our Mental Bags

Tools for the Journey

2

Learning to Be There

A Clash of Cultures

Years ago, I signed up for a summer Hebrew course in Israel so that I'd be able to absorb the sights and sounds of the land as I studied. The class was held at a retreat center a few miles outside Jerusalem, and everywhere you looked you could see evidence of the ancient Israelites.

We'd meet for class all morning, and then the afternoons were dedicated to homework and review. Each day after lunch I'd make a point of hiking into the countryside and doing my homework under a tree, so that I could enjoy the *hoo-hoo-hoot* of the mourning doves and the scent of the cedar trees wafting in the breeze.

These terraced limestone hillsides had been farmed by Israelites thousands of years earlier. A person didn't need to look far to find an ancient basin hewn into the rock where a farmer had once stomped his grapes to press out juice for wine, or a pottery shard from a water jug hefted by a peasant girl in King David's time. Biblical reminders were everywhere. I could just imagine the characters alive around me once again.

Every day, as I headed out after lunch for my favorite tree, I'd walk past a group of college students who were also in my class. They'd cluster tightly in a corner of the air-conditioned reception office, where they'd hang out until supper, hovering over their laptops. After they ate, they'd beeline right back there again. Pretty much every waking hour, that little huddle would convene and glue itself to the chairs.

Why? Because this was the one spot at the retreat center where wireless internet was accessible. (This was in the era before widespread cellphones.) That clique of kids spent the whole summer cruising online and emailing friends at home.

What a tragedy to travel all the way to that fascinating, ancient land, to walk right on its very soil every day, but never once actually "be" there. I'm sure they had the same interest in biblical studies I had, and they had spent as much money to come all this way, but a golden opportunity was passing them right on by.

This brings to mind an interesting rabbinic comment on Exodus 24:12. When God called Moses up to Mount Sinai to receive the tablets of law, what God said, literally, was, "Come up to me on the mountain and *be here*." This seems oddly repetitive. If Moses comes up the mountain, wouldn't he already be there? Translators interpret the text as simply saying that Moses should "wait there." One nineteenth-century rabbi, however, spun a lovely sermon out of the Bible's intriguing choice of words, pointing out that there is, in fact, such a thing as going to a place and not actually being there. He commented,

> If a person exerts himself and ascends to the summit, it is possible to reach it, while not being there. He stands on the summit of the mountain, but his head is somewhere else.[1]

It's entirely possible for a person to expend a great deal of energy getting to a destination, yet arrive there with their head and thoughts remaining at the original point of departure. The rabbi imagined that God was telling Moses not only to ascend the mountain but to be there fully, with complete attention and concentration, leaving behind all of his extraneous thoughts. On the momentous occasion of the giving of the covenant, God wanted Moses to be fully present, in body, mind, and spirit.

I find this very helpful advice for reading the Bible. As you read, do your best to *be there*. In our cellphone-saturated world, some of us need to go into airplane mode and detox awhile so our heads quit buzzing, just so we can think straight.[2]

As wise as this advice is, another aspect of "being there" is an even bigger problem for us. We may be aware of historical differences but we don't think in terms of "being there" with the original audience. The Scriptures are meant for us to read but they were not written to our modern world. God spoke so that the ancient world would understand, as they looked at life through different lenses. If we want to empathize with how they thought and approached life, we need to know more about their culture.

A Clash of Cultures

"Captain, the weather radar has helped us a lot."

These were some of the last recorded words on the black box of a Korean Airlines flight that crashed in Guam in 1997. The copilot was trying to communicate to the pilot that poor visibility had made it too dangerous to attempt to land by sight alone. This was his oblique way of saying that it was imperative they recalculate their approach by relying on their scientific instruments. But thirty seconds later, the 747 crashed into the side of a mountain and more than 250 passengers were killed.

For years the airline industry was perplexed by why certain countries like Korea had a surprisingly high record of plane crashes, despite the fact that the pilots had excellent training and state-of-the-art equipment. Malcolm Gladwell discusses this in his book *Outliers*, which explores unusual reasons why individuals and groups diverge from the majority.[3]

Gladwell explains that the source of the problem turned out to be cultural. Because the task of controlling an airplane is so complex, airplanes are designed to be flown with two pilots. One is in charge of flying while the other cross-checks controls and watches for errors and problems that the pilot might overlook. The system relies on two people pointing out tiny errors that might compound and lead to catastrophe.

This system works well in the United States, which has an egalitarian culture and an open, direct communication style.

But many countries have a stronger sense of hierarchy, where people honor those of greater status by carefully couching their words. To call attention to an error or an overlooked problem in so many words is gallingly rude. In 1990, a Columbian airliner crashed while flying into LaGuardia airport because the copilot was too polite to insist to ground traffic control that they needed to land immediately because they were critically low on fuel.

What was going on was a clash of cultures. The airline industry was designed in America, a society that has a frank, straightforward communication style, not one of cloaked, indirect "hints." Until each country examined its cultural attitudes and trained its pilots to communicate more directly, it continued to face airline disasters.

Nowadays we know that every culture differs from others in basic ways. We expect to encounter very different manners and social expectations when we travel. Even if we meet someone who speaks English, we still might misunderstand each other because of cultural differences. If this is true between us even now, how much more should we expect it as we read our Bibles?

Becoming an Armchair Anthropologist

For me it's become a lifelong project to continually refine my understanding of God's Word in terms of what it meant in its day and then consider the implications for what it means today. Throughout *Reading the Bible with Rabbi Jesus* we'll be exploring many of these ideas more deeply and asking what difference it makes to read the Bible within its own cultural perspective.

One of the key tools I've gained for my toolbox for Bible reading is to be sensitive to how the text might be speaking from a different cultural world than my own. We all need to do this. If we're not listening for differences, we'll tend to fill in the gaps in our Bible reading with our own reality.

When my five-year-old nephew first made the journey from Atlanta to Iowa for Christmas, he marveled at the white fleecy snow that blanketed the tree limbs and buried the bushes. But soon his practical kindergarten brain was cogitating on the implications. With a furrowed brow, he asked his grandpa, "Where do you put the snow when you've got to mow the lawn?" He couldn't fathom an existence where people didn't mow their grass year round and assumed that must be true for us too. As silly as this mistake is, we often do the same with our Bibles. By default we assume that our perspective is universal and project it onto the biblical world.

Or we can make the opposite error and suppose that whatever cultural reality happened to be the setting for the Bible is God's perfect plan for humanity. We piously assume that since it's biblical, it's the way things *ought* to be. Don't forget, though, that God was speaking into a world that had its own harsh realities. Polygamy, concubines, infant sacrifice, and tribal warfare were unfortunate practices of the ancient Near East. The recipients of God's Word were sinners just like us. Despite this, God loved the people of the ancient world and communicated in ways that they could understand. It's not just an intellectual exercise to study the differences between their world and ours. Doing so opens up our Bibles and helps us appreciate God's Word all the more.

More often nowadays people don't see biblical culture as a model to emulate but rather take great offense at it. How dare men have multiple wives and not treat women as equals! How dare the temple exclude lepers for being unclean! We piously snap our Bibles shut out of disgust, not asking how the wider cultural context might have factored in. Or we come up with clever spin to make a passage say the "right" thing—or skip it altogether.

Some are so offended that they feel the Bible should be overhauled. In Robert Funk's *Honest to Jesus*, the founder of the controversial *Jesus Seminar* posted his "Twenty-One Theses" as a nod to Luther's Ninety-Five Theses. Funk's final thesis was that we should

> Declare the New Testament a highly uneven and biased record of the various early attempts to invent Christianity. Reopen the question of what documents belong among the founding witnesses. In a new New Testament, include dissenting opinions. Eliminate the less deserving parts.[4]

As Funk saw it, we need to edit out passages that strike us as wrong and then add better texts. That way we can create an improved Bible that conforms to our own enlightened standards. What a worrisome thought indeed.

The Bible Speaks within Its Context

What I've found over and over is that the Bible doesn't need me to respin or rewrite it, once I grasp its cultural context. When you become aware of it, you often start seeing where the Bible was critiquing the attitudes of its time and calling its audience to live by a higher standard.

For instance, in the biblical world, when a couple married, the wife left her childhood home to join her husband's larger household. Can you imagine how stressful that was? Just as she was establishing a new marriage relationship, she'd also need to adjust to the odd habits and quirky personality of the rest of his family. Laundry? Cooking? They'd have their own way of doing everything. Luckily, her new mother-in-law would be hovering right nearby, ready with advice for each little detail. With this in mind, consider this famous pronouncement in Genesis about marriage:

> That is why a man leaves his father and mother and is united to his wife, and they become one flesh. (Gen. 2:24 NIV)

This line sounds quite backward. Didn't the author know that the woman was the one who'd struggle through the stress of isolation and change? Bible scholar Sandra Richter believes that Genesis is quite intentional in its wording here. She sees it as a subtle comment on marriage in light of the social reality of its time. Of course the woman would leave her home and family for her new husband. But the man needed to shift his loyalties to his new wife too. Richter reads Genesis 2:24 as saying,

> Young man, although you have all the benefits and comforts in this system, from this day onward you shall live your life as if you too have left. She is now bone of your bones and flesh of your flesh. Your most significant kinship alliance, as of today, is her.[5]

Until you place this line from Genesis back into its original setting, you don't appreciate how much wisdom it has for life and for marriage even today.

Putting Our Culture in Perspective

Sometimes the Bible's cultural attitudes can even put our own world into perspective. Do you remember *The Prince of Egypt*? In this animated retelling of the Exodus story, Moses, Miriam, and Aaron all look about twenty-three years old. But have you ever considered the fact that Moses was actually eighty, Aaron was eighty-three, and Miriam was in her mid-nineties? The three dynamic heroes of this action adventure were all senior citizens, old-timers who'd be long out to pasture in our world. Actually, even more of the lead players in the "original cast" of *Prince of Egypt* were seriously over-the-hill by our standards. When Moses came to the leaders of Israel to present God's plan, the ones he approached were the *zakanim*—the elders, or literally, the "beards" of Israel. Throughout the Bible (including the New Testament), elders assumed leadership roles because of the wisdom of their experience.

Advanced age was seen as a sign of God's blessing and a source of honor and dignity. Proverbs 16:31 says, "Gray hair is a crown of splendor; it is attained in the way of righteousness" (NIV), and Job observes, "Is not wisdom found among the aged? Does not long life bring understanding?" (Job 12:12 NIV). Even today, it's an insult in the Middle East to estimate a person's age as too young. Hasidic Jews line the cribs of their newborns with pictures of long-bearded rabbis, who are the "rock stars" of their world.

In the biblical world, youth was seen as a disadvantage. When Jeremiah was first called to be a prophet, he said no because he felt he was too young and therefore no one would listen to him (Jer. 1:6). Likewise, Paul had to encourage his disciple Timothy by saying, "Let no one despise you for your youth" (1 Tim. 4:12). We, on the other hand, idolize young people like Mark Zuckerberg and Justin Beiber. We can hardly imagine living in a world where growing older is actually seen as a *good* thing. What a thought!

"God Has Made Me Fat"

Consider the eye-opening experience some friends of mine had in visiting a church in Mukono, Uganda. It was a Sunday evening, and the women's fellowship group had convened. The women were sharing testimonies, dramatic stories of answered prayer, a tradition they inherited from their evangelistic founders. One woman stood and began by recounting her past life of tribulation: money problems, crop failures, weakness, and ill health. But then the Lord came mightily to her rescue, answering each prayer in turn. As she reached her triumphant conclusion, her voice crescendoed:

"And . . . God . . . has . . . made . . . me . . . fat!"

With a grand flourish she patted her plumpish belly as proof of answered prayer.

You can imagine the chuckling among my American friends who were visiting. Acquiring a few extra pounds is just about the last thing we'd rejoice over. But in Uganda, it's a compliment to tell a friend, "You're looking fat!" There it's a sign of prosperity to put some weight on, because hunger is an ever-present reality.

Believe it or not, the Bible had the same attitude as they do in Uganda about weight gain—that it's a *good* thing, not a bad thing. When the author of the Song of Songs extolled his beloved's beauty, he highlighted her curvaceous, overflowing belly: "Your navel is a rounded goblet that never lacks blended wine. Your waist is a mound of wheat encircled by lilies" (Song of Songs 7:2 NIV).

The biblical world, like most of the world throughout history, struggled against hunger, not flab. Yet there's no end of people who have scoured the Bible for weight-loss secrets. A favorite dieting story is in the first chapter in Daniel, when he and his friends eat only vegetables and drink only water for ten days while the other youths are feasting at the king's table. We resonate with this story of victorious weight loss.

But can I let you in on a little secret?

Daniel's diet plan actually made him fat.

You might miss this if you read the NIV, which says Daniel and his friends were "better nourished" than the young men who ate the royal fare (Dan. 1:15). The Hebrew word that is used here is actually *bari*, which means "fat." The more literal ESV explains that Daniel and his friends had become "*fatter in flesh* than all the youths who ate the king's food" (emphasis added). They hadn't lost weight but rather gained it on Daniel's diet plan! They had expected a diet of only vegetables to leave them thin and weak, but God honored their faithfulness to Jewish dietary law and avoidance of meat sacrificed to idols so that they put on weight instead.

Of course God wants us to be healthy and would be pleased if some of us took off a few excess pounds. But it's important not to extract lessons from the Bible that it never intended to teach. To search the Bible for secrets for slimming down is to read it upside down and backward of what it meant in its time.

Living in Bizzaro World

As a kid, I used to love to read Superman comic books. (Where else can you find a girl named Lois dating a nerd who is actually a hunky superhero in disguise?) One of the planets that Superman would regularly visit was Bizarro World, whose inhabitants purposely did everything backward of how it was done on Earth. They'd say "Goodbye" when someone arrived and "Hello" when they left. They ate supper in the morning and breakfast at night. They pulled flowers out of their gardens and planted weeds. The more I've explored the cultural setting of the Bible, the more I'm convinced that if Abraham visited us today, he'd declare he had landed on Bizarro World:

Our world: Thin is beautiful	Biblical world: Fat is blessing, wealth
Our world: Youth is attractive	Biblical world: Age is wisdom
Our world: Does God exist?	Biblical world: Whose god is greatest?
Our world: Me—personal goals	Biblical world: We—family legacy
Our world: Sunshine—happiness	Biblical world: Rain—utter joy
Our world: Logic and reason	Biblical world: Parable and prophecy

Why is our perspective so different? Obviously, thousands of years of time separate us. But there might be another reason for our difficulty. Eugene Nida traveled the globe to oversee Bible translation projects in over eighty countries during his four-decade career with the American Bible Society. As a linguist and Bible translator, he encountered more cultures than anyone else who ever lived. Surprisingly, he believed that much of the world has less difficulty understanding the Bible than modern Americans. He writes:

> In a sense, the Bible is the most translatable religious book that has ever been written, for it comes from a particular time

> and place (the western end of the Fertile Crescent) through which passed more cultural patterns and out from which radiated more distinctive features and values than any other place in the history of the world.
>
> If one were to make a comparison of the culture traits of the Bible with those of all the existing cultures of today . . . one would find that in certain respects the Bible is surprisingly closer to many of them than to the technological culture of the western world. It is this "western" culture that is the aberrant one in the world. And it is precisely in the western world, and in the growing number of persons in other parts of the world, that the Scriptures have seemingly the least ready acceptance.[6]

What an interesting thought—that much of the world finds the Bible less difficult to read than we do. I had heard this sentiment already from my African friends, with their "biblical" feelings about weight loss.

I've since heard similar statements from Native Americans and readers in China: often the cultural issues we have with the Bible are not a problem for people elsewhere in the world. They've struggled with the Christian message as they've heard it filtered through the perspective of Western missionaries, but when it's explained in its original non-Western setting, it makes much more sense to them.[7]

I was chatting with another Ugandan friend about the line in Deuteronomy when God tells his people to "Talk about [my commandments] when you sit at home and when you walk along the road, when you lie down and when you get up" (6:7 NIV). I wondered why it says, "when you walk along the road." Because, my friend explained, much of people's time was likely spent walking, traveling on foot for every journey. Where she grew up, she'd walk for hours or days at a time. Jesus' five-day journey from Nazareth to Jerusalem seemed not unreasonable to her. (This, of course, is yet another reason why the Bible contains no weight-loss plans.)

I'm Feeling a Little WEIRD

In 2010, a groundbreaking paper in psychology revealed an intriguing clue. Researchers had noticed that European and American responses to psychological studies were often far from typical compared with the rest of the world. So they did a comparison of cultural attitudes and differences between various populations across the globe. In several aspects, Americans were at the far end of the spectrum. Psychologists coined the acronym "WEIRD" for the attitudes of Euro/American culture (particularly the secular university world) that were consistently different from the rest of humanity. We are

Western
Educated
Industrialized
Rich
Democratic (in voting countries)[8]

What I find fascinating is that these same traits often set our culture apart from the Middle Eastern reality of Jesus and the biblical world. Let's just consider how WEIRD cultural traits contrast with how the Bible "thinks."

Western and Educated

We formulate ideas as our Greek cultural ancestors did, not as the biblical Hebrews of Jesus' world and heritage did. We think in abstractions and find proof-based logical argument far more convincing than the parables Jesus used.

As children of the Enlightenment, we have seen the power of human reason conquer the physical world and are convinced that human reason is the measure of all things. Science is the final proof of truth in our way of thinking.

Industrialized

The rhythms of our lives have been utterly transformed by modernity. We don't sustain ourselves on the land by working alongside family through seasons of planting and harvest. Jesus' frequent parables about fishermen and farmers don't evoke a visceral response in us, as they did in his agrarian world. We derive our basic identity from our work outside of the home, not from the growth and strength of our family.

Rich

Most of us are relatively "rich" in that we have easy access to food and housing and feel somewhat secure about our future, or at least our survival. The daily worries of people throughout history simply don't concern us.

When we read Jesus' parable in Luke 12:15–21 about a farmer who builds barns for a bumper crop so that he can retire to the easy life, we wonder what the problem is. His behavior actually fits quite well into a WEIRD culture, where he'd be praised for having the forethought to "pay himself first" and create the biblical equivalent of a Roth IRA. In much of the world, it would be shocking that the farmer didn't share his windfall with his community.

Democratic

We are used to government being "by the people, for the people," and we place a strong emphasis on individualism and independence. We define ourselves in terms of our rights and freedoms. By contrast, much of the world doesn't see personal autonomy as an important value. Rather, they view people principally as members of groups—families, tribes, and nations—that make strong claims on the people's loyalty. What defines you are your relationships, and what orders your life are your responsibilities to others, not your personal freedom to do what you like.

You might wonder, why this amazing coincidence? Why should traits that set apart Euro/Americans in psychological studies overlap with cultural differences between us and the Bible? Well, consider Eugene Nida's comment that our technological Western culture is unusual relative to the rest of the world. If our cultural "boat" has been drifting away from the common perspective of humankind, it shouldn't be so surprising that the same traits that make us unique are attitudes that make it hard for us to understand our Bibles. *We're* the ones who have shifted, relative to others.

Phillip Jenkins, historian and author of *The Next Christendom: The Coming of Global Christianity*, comments:

> For many Americans and Europeans, not only are the societies in the Bible—in both testaments—distant in terms of time and place, but their everyday assumptions are all but

> incomprehensible. Yet exactly the issues that make the Bible a distant historical record for many Americans and Europeans keep it a living text in the churches of the global South. . . . And this identification extends to the Old Testament no less than the New.[9]

I find this somewhat comforting, actually. I used to wonder why God would let the Bible become difficult for humanity to understand. It really hasn't, at least in the global South (Africa, Asia, and Latin America), where the church has been expanding rapidly, according to Jenkins. North America and Europe are the places where the biblical message is most unacceptable, where we least resonate with the narrative of Scripture. *We're* the ones who have a hard time getting the point.

What might the rest of the world know that we need to understand?

How the Bible "Thinks"

Throughout this book, we'll take a closer look at how the Bible "thinks" and the assumptions it makes that are very different from those we make today. I'm not talking about the usual pious way we speak of "thinking more biblically" in terms of being more loving and Christlike. I'm talking about imagining how the biblical world approached life differently than we do and how God spoke into that world on its own terms.

Of course I'm speaking in generalizations, and generalizations are always wrong when overextended. Some may apply more to Abraham or David than Jesus. They should be helpful even if they are approximate. They will still bring you closer to the New Testament world than the world we live in today.

TOOLS AND REFLECTIONS

Reading

1. Read Acts 1:4–8 and 2:1–8. In these passages about the mission of the disciples and Pentecost, what was the mission that Jesus called his disciples to take on? (See Matt. 28:19–20 too.) At Pentecost, how did the Spirit empower them to do it? What are some of the ways you'd need to be equipped to bring the message across the globe?

2. What aspects of biblical society (in the Old or New Testament) do you struggle with most? What things have changed for the better since then?

3. In order to "be there," we need to travel across both time and culture. What aspects of our WEIRD culture separate us most from the biblical world, as you see it?

4. In a group discussion, ask members with international backgrounds (or those who have spent time overseas) if they can comment on the oddest cultural things they've had to adjust to. What aspects of WEIRDness do they especially notice?

Thoughts for Going Deeper

- Make a habit of befriending people from other cultures and discussing the differences that they see between their perspective and your own. Invite them to a Bible study and ask them for their input as you study. My Ugandan friends have had a wealth of insights to share with me, not because they have any more direct knowledge of the biblical world than I do but simply because they provide a perspective from a culture unlike mine.

- Also, talk to missionaries or Bible translators who have encountered a world unlike their own and have taught the Bible there. Often they come back with all sorts of insights that they've learned from the very people whom they are trying to teach.
- A truly great little book for understanding cultural differences is Sarah Lanier's *Foreign to Familiar: A Guide to Understanding Hot- and Cold-Climate Cultures* (Hagerstown, MD: McDougal Publishing, 2000). I guarantee you will like this brief, helpful guide.
- Check out these excellent books on how culture influences how we read the Bible:

  E. Randolph Richards and Brandon J. O'Brien, *Misunderstanding Scripture with Western Eyes: Removing Cultural Blinders to Better Understand the Bible* (Downers Grove, IL: Intervarsity Press, 2012)

  Jackson Wu, *One Gospel for all Nations: A Practical Approach to Biblical Contextualization* (Pasadena, CA: William Carey Library, 2015)

3

What Does "Christ" Mean, Anyway?

A Perplexing Word

Jesus' question at Emmaus rang in my ears: "Was it not necessary that the Christ should suffer these things and enter into his glory?" He seemed incredulous that the disciples he had met that day had been so thickheaded about his mission. Then he walked them from beginning to end through the Scriptures, reviewing what was expected of the Christ and how he had fulfilled those expectations.

It was a little embarrassing. As clueless as those disciples were that day, I was even more of a dunce. Despite a straight-A Sunday school career, I needed to start a step or two earlier with an even more basic question: What exactly is a *Christ*, anyhow?

What did that word actually mean? Where did people find it in their Scriptures? What did first-century Jews expect of this glorious figure? I had been speaking of Jesus as "Christ" all my life, loosely equating it with Jesus being my Savior but never asking what it meant in its original cultural setting. It wasn't until I peered at the concept of the word *Christ* under the lens of ancient context that I started to notice its surprising imagery and see its important implications.

Studying this one word in its culture was what began to unlock the rest of the Bible to me. Excavating the original promises about the coming Christ was just the beginning of my amazing journey into the Scriptures that continues to this day.

Over and over I discovered that when I read the Bible through the eyes of a first-century listener, the earth-shattering ideas I found in the New Testament had deep and winding roots in the ancient soil of the Scriptures that Jesus read.

The Anointed One

First of all, the word *Christ* comes from *christos*, a Greek word meaning "anointed." It is the equivalent of the word *mashiach*, or *Messiah*, in Hebrew. So, to be the Christ, or Messiah, is to be "the anointed of God." But what does that mean?

To be anointed, literally, is to have sacred oil poured on one's head, usually to appoint a person to a holy office. This widespread custom stretches far back into history. The ancient Egyptians anointed their high officials, and the Hittites appointed their kings with the "holy oil of kingship" at their coronation. In Israel, high priests were anointed, as well as kings like Saul, David, and Solomon. Several times in the Scriptures God told a prophet to go anoint someone and proclaim him king.[1]

During the reign of Israel's great monarchs we first start hearing the phrase "anointed one" (*mashiach*) regularly, and from then on it was most often used to refer to a *king*. David used this term many times to refer to King Saul, even when Saul was bent on hunting down David and killing him. Listen to what David exclaimed after he encountered Saul in a cave and his men urged him to assassinate him:

> The LORD forbid that I should do such a thing to my master, the LORD's anointed [*mashiach*], or lay my hand on him; for he is the anointed [*mashiach*] of the LORD. (1 Sam. 24:6 NIV)

The act of anointing with sacred oil emphasized that it was *God himself* who had ordained a person and given him authority to lead his people and act as his representative. That's why David wouldn't lay a hand on Saul. Saul had been appointed by God as king, and no human being was worthy to unseat him. Priests were anointed too—and prophets, rarely. So the most prominent idea within the title "Christ" is actually that of a *king*. In simple terms, we could say that "Jesus Christ" means, "Jesus, God's chosen King."

Is this what you would have guessed? Twenty years ago, I remember being quite dumbfounded by this discovery. If I had been asked to take a guess at what "Christ" meant before looking it up, I would have said something like "God incarnate" or "divine Savior" or "one who died for my sins." I was actually quite shocked by "anointed King." It didn't even make my list.

The whole "king" idea might seem utterly foreign to the life of a humble Galilean rabbi. But the more I studied ancient ideas about royalty, the more I found them popping up in the Gospels. They are clearest at the beginning and the end of his life. At Jesus' birth, when the wise men visited Herod, they asked, "Where is he who has been born king of the Jews?" (Matt. 2:2). The chief priests informed Herod that he'd be born in Bethlehem, because Micah had prophesied that a ruler would arise from Bethlehem, where King David had been born:

> But you, Bethlehem Ephrathah, though you are small among the clans of Judah, out of you will come for me one who will be ruler over Israel, whose origins are from of old, from ancient times. (Mic. 5:2 NIV)

Later, at the end of Jesus' life, during his trial, the main question that he was asked was "Are you the King of the Jews?" which he answered affirmatively:

> And they began to accuse Him, saying, "We found this man misleading our nation and forbidding to pay taxes to Caesar, and saying that He Himself is Christ, a King." So Pilate asked Him, saying, "Are You the King of the Jews?" And He answered him and said, "It is as you say." (Luke 23:2–3 NASB)

If you think that these couple of references are the only places in the Gospels where you see kingship being associated with Jesus, it's because you're unaware, as I was, of all the cultural imagery associated with kingship in the ancient world. You also need to know some significant events in the history of Israel.

Hints of a Coming King

As I dug deeper, I discovered hints sprinkled throughout the Scriptures that God would send a great King to Israel. The clearest prophecy about this figure comes from King David's time. David earnestly desired to build a temple, a "house" for God, but God responded that his son Solomon would be the one to build his temple. God then promised that he would build a "house" for David, meaning that God would establish his family line after him. He further promised that from David's family would come a King whose kingdom would have no end:

> When your days are over and you go to be with your ancestors, I will raise up your offspring to succeed you, one of your own sons, and I will establish his kingdom. He is the one who will build a house for me, and I will establish his throne forever. I will be his father, and he will be my son. I will never take my love away from him, as I took it away from your predecessor. I will set him over my house and my kingdom forever; his throne will be established forever. (1 Chron. 17:11–14 NIV)

This prophecy has been understood as having a double fulfillment. It was first fulfilled in Solomon, who built the temple but did what God forbade—amassed a great fortune and married foreign wives. His kingdom broke apart a few years after his death. But this prophecy looks forward to a "Son of David" who would have a kingdom without end. Christians can't miss God's remarkable words about him: "I will be his father, and he will be my son" (v. 13 NIV). This "Son of David" would be the Son of God!

This, in fact, is the primal seedbed of all of the messianic prophecies that speak of the coming of Christ, God's promised King. During Israel's low times, during the exile and afterward, the prophets gave the people hope through wonderful visions of a future deliverer of Israel. Sometimes this figure was even called "David" because his reign would continue David's legacy. In Ezekiel's visions of the glorious future, he promised, "My servant David shall be king over them, and they shall all have one shepherd. . . . David my servant shall be their prince forever" (Ezek. 37:24–25).

Looking further back into Israel's Scriptures, we hear hints that suggest this future King will be far more than just sovereign over Israel. In Genesis 49, Jacob blessed each of his sons who would become the forefathers of the twelve tribes of Israel. There he foretold that from the tribe of Judah one would come who would reign over the whole world:

> The scepter shall not depart from Judah,
> nor the ruler's staff from between his feet,
> until tribute comes to him;
> and to him shall be the obedience of the peoples.
> (Gen. 49:10)

Echoes from the Life of Solomon

Because Solomon was David's literal son who was a great king, events from his life became expectations of what the messianic King would be like. For instance, look at how Solomon was crowned as king over Israel. When King David had grown infirm, his oldest son, Adonijah, decided to announce himself as Israel's next king. Adonijah was right in the middle of throwing a grand party to celebrate his reign when David gave the prophet Nathan these instructions:

> Take with you the servants of your lord and have Solomon my son ride on my own mule, and bring him down to Gihon. And let Zadok the priest and Nathan the prophet there anoint him king over Israel. Then blow the trumpet and say, "Long live King Solomon!" You shall then come up after him, and he shall come and sit on my throne, for he shall be king in my place. (1 Kings 1:33–35)

The fact that Solomon was seated on David's own mule telegraphed to the crowds that he was the one who had his father's blessing, because use of the king's personal property was strictly prohibited. By being seated on David's mount, it was as if he was already seated on his throne.

Later on, the prophet Zechariah foresees the arrival of the Messiah the same way:

> Rejoice greatly, O daughter of Zion!
> Shout aloud, O daughter of Jerusalem!
> Behold, your king is coming to you;
> righteous and having salvation is he,
> humble and mounted on a donkey,
> on a colt, the foal of a donkey. (Zech. 9:9)

This was the message the crowds heard in Jesus' life too, when he entered Jerusalem on a donkey. Everyone recognized the significance. Here was the true Son of David. The crowds shouted, "Blessed is he who comes in the name of the Lord, even the King of Israel!" (John 12:13). John's Gospel tells us that the night before Jesus' triumphal entry in Jerusalem, in Bethany, he was even anointed by Mary. The parallels were inescapable. We need to know Israel's history to see how Jesus was bringing it to fulfillment.

Gifts Fit for a King

Other events in Solomon's life shed light on events that occur during the Gospels. Consider what happened when the Queen of Sheba paid him a visit:

> Now when the queen of Sheba heard of the fame of Solomon concerning the name of the LORD, she came to test him with hard questions. She came to Jerusalem with a very great retinue, with camels bearing spices and very much gold and precious stones. And when she came to Solomon, she told him all that was on her mind. And Solomon answered all her questions; there was nothing hidden from the king that he could not explain to her. . . . Then she gave the king 120 talents of gold, and a very great quantity of spices and precious stones. Never again came such an abundance of spices as these that the queen of Sheba gave to King Solomon. (1 Kings 10:1–3, 10)

Do you see the similarity between this story and the visit of the wise men in Matthew 2, when they brought gold, frankincense, and myrrh? In both accounts, visitors from distant lands came with expensive gifts to show friendliness toward a powerful new king.

The connections are even closer if you know a few more historical details. Sheba was at the southern end of the Arabian peninsula, where Yemen is today, about 1,800 miles from Israel. In ancient times it was known for possessing fabulous wealth. Frankincense and myrrh were some of its most precious exports. Notice that the queen traveled by camel. For millennia, camels have been used for transporting luxury goods along the spice trade routes of the Mediterranean because they are the only animals that can survive the dangerously dry Arabian desert. With these details in mind, consider these prophecies about the messianic King:

> May he have dominion from sea to sea,
> and from the River to the ends of the earth!
> May desert tribes bow down before him,
> and his enemies lick the dust!
> May the kings of Tarshish and of the coastlands
> render him tribute;
> may the kings of Sheba and Seba
> bring gifts!
> May all kings fall down before him,
> all nations serve him!
> Long may he live;
> may gold of Sheba be given to him!
> (Ps. 72:8–11, 15)

> Nations will come to your light,
> and kings to the brightness of your dawn. . . .
> The wealth on the seas will be brought to you,
> to you the riches of the nations will come.
> Herds of camels will cover your land,
> young camels of Midian and Ephah.
> And all from Sheba will come,
> bearing gold and incense
> and proclaiming the praise of the Lord.
> (Isa. 60:3, 5–6 NIV)

Have you ever wondered why Christmas carols sing about "we three kings" and picture Jesus' visitors coming on camels, even though Matthew 2 doesn't mention either detail? Over the ages, Christian readers saw that Matthew's account echoed Psalm 72:10, which pictures kings from Tarshish, Sheba, and Seba paying tribute to the future messiah. They inferred that the visitors were actually royalty from each of these three countries.

Why, then, do we find "wise men" instead of kings in the New Testament? Likely because they were acting as ambassadors (1 Kings 4:34). In the ancient world, kings often employed royal counselors who had been schooled in magical arts like divination and astrology. Recall Pharaoh's magicians, who imitated Moses' miracles, and Nebuchadnezzar's wise men and dream interpreters. When these counselors in distant lands determined that a powerful ruler had arisen in Israel, they were sent as royal emissaries to pay tribute on behalf of their leaders.

The Puzzle of the Gospel

The most surprising discovery I made about ancient kingship is that I had been misunderstanding the word *gospel* throughout the New Testament. I knew that *gospel* meant "good news" and, like most, assumed that the good news is that we have forgiveness of sins because of Jesus' sacrifice for us on the cross.

But, in fact, the Greek word for gospel, *euanggelion* (literally, "good news"), in the New Testament also comes from terminology that was used in regards to kings and their dominions. When a new king was crowned, the *euanggelion* was the announcement that the monarch had taken the throne, that a new kingdom had taken power.

Why is this called "good news"? Because an announcement of *euanggelion* was good news to the empire and its cheering citizens, even though enemies and dissidents would find it quite terrible. How happy you are as the hearer is not the point. The news is good for the king and his kingdom.

Strictly speaking, the gospel, the *euanggelion*, is simply that God had appointed Jesus as his chosen King. This was why Paul was utterly focused on preaching the "*euanggelion* of Christ" and spoke of himself as his "ambassador" to the Gentile world.

How does Jesus being the promised King of Israel have anything to do with us being saved from our sins? This is even more of a puzzler. But shortly after his Emmaus conversation, in Jesus' very next appearance that evening, he says that this is exactly the case:

> Thus it is written, that the Christ should suffer and on the third day rise from the dead, and that repentance for the forgiveness of sins should be proclaimed in his name to all nations, beginning from Jerusalem. (Luke 24:46–47)

Whew! The gospel as we've always preached it is indeed linked to the *euanggelion* as Jesus understood it. Originally, the "goodness" of the *euanggelion* was in the fact that it announced God's anointed King had come and had even been raised from the dead. Yet it is indeed connected to the fact that we can be forgiven of our sins. But how?

According to Jesus, the answer is staring us right in the face in his Scriptures, our Old Testament. Does that surprise you? Certainly we find this written all over the New Testament, but where do we find this answer in the Old Testament? What clues can we find to help us read the Bible the way he did? In the last section of the book, we'll look specifically at this question.

But Kings Just Aren't Good News

Excavating the imagery of ancient kingship helped me solve several mysteries in Jesus' life, yet it created even more. When I told one friend that *euanggelion* was about Jesus as King, she responded, "Well, that isn't very good news! I don't want a king!"

Some of us find the whole idea of kings and kingdoms obnoxious. In the church where I grew up, every new hymnal that came out was increasingly scrubbed free of words like these. Instead of praying "thy kingdom come," it's "thy wisdom come" or "may your reality be honored."

Could it be that the "D" in WEIRD, which stands for "democratic," is coloring our understanding? We live in an egalitarian society that emphasizes personal autonomy, freedom, and individual rights. We expect to have a vote in every decision that affects us. So we bristle at submitting to any kind of authority, to the point where central biblical metaphors like God establishing his "kingdom" on earth and the Messiah as God's anointed "King" simply do not resonate. To the contrary, this imagery may actually *offend* us.

Some of us are so pained by a bombastic, tyrannical title like "king" that we automatically assume the humble sage from Galilee would reject it outright. Yet we see him riding on a donkey into Jerusalem to the cheers of the crowds, and at Emmaus we find him discussing his mission as the Christ.

Could our problem be cultural? Rather than objecting and discarding the idea of kingship outright, what if we lingered a little longer in this foreign world, long enough to see if our assumptions about this imagery are even correct?

We've already encountered several ideas about kingship in the ancient world that shed light on the life of Jesus. Maybe we'll learn some other things along the way.

Longing for a Judge?

If the "king" idea doesn't bother you, other ideas associated with kings might. Like the fact that kings in ancient times were also expected to act as judges.

An essential function of a king was as the supreme judge in the land. Before Israel had kings, its leaders were called "judges," and kings took on this role too. When Solomon built his throne room, the text describes it this way: "He made the Hall of the Throne where he was to pronounce judgment, even the Hall of Judgment" (1 Kings 7:7).

A king was charged with establishing a just society by destroying the corruption and exploitation within it. Indeed, in Hebrew, the word for "judgment," *mishpat* (meesh-PAHT), also means "justice." By judging wrongdoers, a king was establishing justice in the land. Listen to the messianic imagery of Psalm 72:

> Give the king your justice, O God,
> and your righteousness to the royal son!

May he judge your people with righteousness,
and your poor with justice! (vv. 1–2)

This is another reason why kings don't sound terribly good to us. Would you believe that to many, this would be very good news? Consider the talk that Gary Haugen, founder of International Justice Mission, gave at the 2015 TED conference. He told the story of Venus, a young mother of two in Zambia who watched her younger son starve to death. "We were doing fine," Venus told him, "until Brutus started to cause trouble."

Haugen goes on, "Now, Brutus is Venus's neighbor, and 'cause trouble' is what happened the day after Venus's husband died, when Brutus just came and threw Venus and the kids out of the house, stole all their land, and robbed their market stall. You see, Venus was thrown into destitution by violence."[2] The reason for this woman's poverty was not that she didn't have land and a way to grow food and make money . . . at least at one time. It was because she had no one to go to who would bring Brutus to justice.

Imagine what it would be like to live in a world where there are no police, where the weak are perpetual victims of any bully who finds them. This may sound unthinkable, but everyday violence is a massive problem in the developing world today, according to Haugen. Over two billion people live in countries that have woefully inadequate law enforcement. In impoverished areas, there is often no credible criminal deterrent, nothing to prevent the vulnerable from being victimized by bullies and thieves.[3]

Listen to a few more lines of Psalm 72 and consider for a moment why widows like Venus might appreciate them:

> May he defend the cause of the poor of the people,
> give deliverance to the children of the needy,
> and crush the oppressor! . . .
> For he delivers the needy when he calls,
> the poor and him who has no helper.
> He has pity on the weak and the needy,
> and saves the lives of the needy.
> From oppression and violence he redeems their life,
> and precious is their blood in his sight.
> (vv. 4, 12–14)

Psalm 72 is a prayer for the messianic King that frames his role as one who brings bullies to judgment. Many, however, are pained by its violent plea to "crush the oppressor" (v. 4). In a visceral way, though, I can imagine widows praying daily for this kind of redemption. They'd long for the day when the Messiah would establish a kingdom in which justice reigns and the weakest could live without fear.

Indeed, it was understood that *kings themselves* would stand before the King of Kings as their judge. One psalm from about a century before Christ puts it this way:

> Hear then, you kings, take this to heart; learn your lesson, lords of the wide world; lend your ears, you rulers of the multitude. . . . Though you are viceroys of his kingly power, you have not been upright judges; you do not stand up for the law or guide your steps by the will of God. Swiftly and terribly will he descend upon you, for judgment falls relentlessly upon those in high places. The small man may find pity and forgiveness, but the powerful will be called powerfully to account.[4]

I wonder if it would make a difference to our president and the rest of the world's leaders if they knew that someday they'd stand before Christ and have to account for themselves.

It seems like a cultural gap separates us from a world that longs for a mighty ruler. Living in a safe society, we can't relate to this widespread longing for protection and justice. We read biblical imagery and call it "primitive" and "violent" because we have little concept of the harsh reality that many in the world endure even now.

Don't Just Analyze, Empathize

I began this book with imagery that surrounds the title "Christ" because it is so central to the biblical story yet so foreign to us. Throughout the book we will find many more ways that messianic imagery can teach us about Jesus' life and mission. More importantly, we'll see how he challenged and redefined the expectations surrounding this key image.

You don't need to live in a lawless society in order to appreciate Psalm 72. But you do need to be able to mentally bridge the gap between our world and that world in order to empathize with how they saw life. My goal is not to make you feel you need to adopt the lifestyle of the biblical world but to help you be willing to view life through its lens for just a little while.

Don't just analyze and take notes on cultural differences. Try your best to mentally place yourself in that reality long enough to look around and see its internal logic. Resonate with the people who were there and read the Bible through their eyes. Then bring it back to your own world, which may be very different.

We live on the other side of Pentecost from Emmaus, and our commission is to make disciples of all nations. The first thing God did when he poured out his Spirit at Pentecost was make his disciples into *translators*. Translating language is only part of it—we need to translate culture too.

Translators need to be deeply fluent in two languages. They will tell you that, at a certain point, it feels like their brain is "split" between two different ways of thinking. To translate, they have to mentally leap between worlds and then bridge that gap for others. That's what we need to do between the culture of the biblical world and our own.

TOOLS AND REFLECTIONS

Reading

1. The kings of the united monarchy of Israel were Saul, David, Solomon, and Rehoboam. Read 1 Samuel 8:1–20, about when the Israelites first wanted a king after having priests in leadership. What were they warned? Read 2 Chronicles 10:1–16. What happened during the reign of Rehoboam?

2. Read Deuteronomy 17:14–20. What aspects of these laws describe Jesus and his kingdom? How did Solomon, the first "son of David," do at observing these laws? See 1 Kings 11:1–8.

3. Read the prophet Isaiah's vision of the messianic King in Isaiah 11:1–9 and 42:1–7. How does the Messiah as

Isaiah envisions him compare to Jesus, as opposed to earlier kings?

4. Read 1 Kings 1:33–40 and John 12:3–13. What similarities do you see between these stories? What might the anointing and the rest of the scene be saying about Jesus?

Thoughts for Going Deeper

- Whenever you see the word "Christ" in the New Testament, try stubstituting "God's chosen King" and reading the text in that light.
- Whenever your Bible sounds offensive to you, step back and ask if there could be something going on in the culture you don't know about. Try your best to "be there."
- Consider the perspective of your great-grandparents. Sometimes our cultural difficulties with the Bible are those of modernity. Even a few decades ago a king was a more familiar, positive image.
- For more about the conversation about the "kingdom of God" that was going on in first-century Judaism and how it relates to Jesus as Messiah, see *Sitting at the Feet of Rabbi Jesus* (Spangler and Tverberg, Zondervan, 2009), 180–96.
- There are also several chapters about Jesus' Jewish teachings on the kingdom of God in Brad Young's *Jesus the Jewish Theologian* (Hendrickson, 1995). Also helpful is N. T. Wright's *How God Became King* (Harper Collins, 2012).

4

Painting in Hebrew

Bold Colors, Broad Brushstrokes

Every few months or so, a new Bible translation marches across Christian bookstore shelves. The English Standard Version . . . the International Standard Version . . . the New International Version . . . the Revised Standard Version . . . the Modern Revised Version . . . and on and on and on. Why are there so many Bibles? Why can't we just have one final, best translation and call it a day?

You might assume there's a conspiracy going on, but a major reason why we haven't settled on a single Bible translation actually comes from an aspect of language that most of us don't think about. When you speak, you "paint," in a sense. You choose from a list of words in your language that have the hues and overtones you're looking for and you blend them into sentences to express what you mean. Each language is a palette with a finite amount of colors. When you try to paint a scene in a different language, the same words carry different shades of meaning, so the result is never exactly the same.

This is especially true when translating between Hebrew and English, and less so with Greek. Greek and English have relatively close palettes because both languages grew out of the same Indo-European roots, and many English words originally came from Greek. Hebrew, however, reflects a very different Afro-Asiatic heritage. It is tinged by the desert browns and burnt umbers of a Semitic, earthy tribe who trekked through parched wastelands, ate manna, herded sheep, and slung stones at their enemies.

Hebrew also contains a smaller set of "pigments" than English—about eight thousand words, in comparison to one hundred thousand or more in our language.[1] Martin Luther noticed this from his work in Bible translation. He commented:

> The Hebrew tongue, above other languages, is very plain, but withal it is majestic and glorious: it contains much in few and simple words, and therein surpasses all other languages.[2]

You could say that Hebrew expresses truth by splashing on bold colors with a broad brush, like van Gogh. Even though the details are quite rough, you mentally fill them in, inferring them from the context. Your mind is used to figuring out meaning from context. Even in English we sketch out a scene with a few "word strokes" and let listeners figure out the rest. Instantly we recognize the difference between getting a run in baseball, getting a run in your stocking, and getting a run in after work.

Imagine yourself as a Bible translator who is "repainting" a scene into English. If you aim to translate word-for-word, you can only use one stroke of your brush to portray each stroke in the original. But you have to trade your wide Hebrew "brush" for a fine-tipped English "brush," and your color palette isn't quite the same. English may have more hues to choose from, but each stroke can pick up only one overtone within the original swath of color.

What will you do?

Most likely, the result of your efforts will show people the overall scene but it won't quite capture the atmosphere of the original. Another translator would bring out different shades and overtones from the exact same text. Certainly, some renderings will be better than others, but it simply isn't possible to perfectly reproduce a painting with a different palette and different brushes. This is why there will never be one solitary, "best" translation of the Bible that replaces all others.[3]

What's a person to do, then, to get the truest sense of the original text? Rather than clinging to one translation, you'll actually get a clearer idea if you read from more than one version and then compare them. Read from a few major translations that aim to be more word-for-word and then look at some that are more thought-for-thought. When you see the range of ways that artists "paint" the same passage, you'll start to get a better sense of the colorful hues within the original. (More about this at the end of the chapter.)

God's "Heart" Language

Along with using multiple translations, another set of tools that will greatly aid in encountering the Scriptures as Jesus' first disciples did is to familiarize yourself with some of the Bible's Hebrew words.

Why Hebrew? Well, Hebrew is God's heart language—the mother tongue of the Scriptures Jesus read. Hebrew is an extremely rich, poetic language that looks at the world in very different ways than English. Grasping the depth of even a few words greatly clarifies and enriches reading and casts new light on things that you *thought* you understood.[4]

Hebrew is helpful for reading not just the Old Testament but the New Testament too. Although the New Testament was written in Greek, it was composed almost entirely by Jews growing up in a Semitic-thinking culture. Often Hebrew's deep, rich pigments diffuse through, showing evidence of the writer's original "accent."

Take, for instance, the word *walk*, which in biblical Hebrew is *halakh* (ha-LAKH) and is widely used as a metaphor to describe one's moral lifestyle, as in Psalm 1:1, "Blessed is the man who does not *walk* in the counsel of the wicked" (NASB). In Greek this is normally not the case. The word for *walk* is *peripateo*, and it simply means "to stroll around" or "travel on foot." Yet the New Testament often uses it with a Hebraic sense instead. Jesus was asked why his disciples did not "walk" according to the tradition of the elders (Mark 7:5), and Paul exhorted the Thessalonians to "walk" in order to please God (1 Thess. 4:1). A Greek reader would have scratched his head at why Paul wanted his listeners to "stroll around to please God." It's only when we recognize Paul's Jewish, Hebraic accent that his intent becomes clear.[5]

Once again, Martin Luther shares a wise thought with us:

> If I were young, I would contrive a way and means for the perfect learning of the Hebrew tongue, which is both glorious and profitable, and without which the Holy Scriptures

> cannot rightly be understood; for although the New Testament be written in Greek, yet it is full of the Hebrew kind of speaking, from whence it is truly said, "The Hebrews drink out of the fountain, the Grecians out of the springs that flow from the fountain; the Latins out of the ponds."[6]

Spacious Suitcases

Another way of looking at language is to see it as the luggage in which we "package" our thoughts in order to transport them into the minds of others. In English, we have an enormous number of "suitcases" we can use—words with various shades of meaning and formality. You might wonder how Hebrew can communicate with fewer words. The reason is that each "suitcase" is roomier inside—deeper, wider, more spacious. Many Hebrew words carry a wider range of meaning than the corresponding word in English.

Unpacking the ideas within a Hebrew "suitcase" is often enormously helpful in Bible study. It's a delightful exercise in seeing how the ancient authors organized ideas in very different ways than we do—when they used the same word for "work" as for "worship" and the same word for "listen" and "obey."

We English speakers are used to very precise meanings, and we expect to have everything carefully defined. But Hebrew words leave the listener to discern the meaning from the context. The prophets and other biblical writers actually seemed to delight in pondering the nuances of their language. They often made wordplays based on a word's ambiguity, deliberately invoking multiple layers of a word's meaning.

For instance, the word *ruach* (roo-AKH) means "breath," "wind," or "spirit." When God's *ruach* blows through the Valley of Dry Bones to bring new life in Ezekiel 37, we see that *all* of its various meanings are intended. Jesus was also aware of these facets of *ruach* when he declared,

> No one can enter the kingdom of God unless they are born of water and the Spirit. Flesh gives birth to flesh, but the Spirit gives birth to spirit. You should not be surprised at my saying, "You must be born again." The wind blows wherever it pleases. You hear its sound, but you cannot tell where it comes from or where it is going. So it is with everyone born of the Spirit. (John 3:5–8 NIV)

I've always imagined that God chose to reveal his Word in Hebrew because the language invites us to think more deeply. As we read the Scriptures, we ask God what he is saying to us again and again.

To Fear or Be in Awe?

Take the word *yirah* (YEER-ah), for instance, which is usually translated as "fear." The word *fear* is common in the Old Testament, and to many it sounds like we should cringe in dread of God. Of course, we find "fear" in the New Testament too. The Gentiles who believed in God were called God-fearers, and the early church was said to be built up in the "fear of the Lord" (Acts 9:31). Why is there so much fear in the Bible?

To solve this mystery, you need to know more about the Hebrew word for fear, *yirah*. Our English word *fear* narrowly focuses on being afraid. To us, fear is the opposite of trust and is synonymous with worry, dread, or fright. But *yirah* encompasses a much wider range of meanings, from negative (dread, terror) to positive (worship, reverence) and from mild (respect) to strong (awe).

Whenever you read "revere" or "reverence" in your Bible, the word *yirah* is most likely behind it. In Leviticus 19:3, we are told to "*yirah*" (revere) our mother and father, and in verse 30 to "Keep my Sabbaths and reverence [*yirah*] my sanctuary." In both places *yirah* is not about being afraid but rather showing honor and veneration.

When we see the phrase "fear of God," Christians sometimes focus on fearing the punishment that God could give us for our deeds. Certainly, we'll all stand before God's judgment seat when we die. But if you know that Christ has paid for your sins, you shouldn't have this kind of fear anymore. This is what John preaches against when he says, "There is no fear in love; but perfect love casts out fear, because fear involves punishment, and the one who fears is not perfected in love" (1 John 4:18 NASB).

Yet the Bible speaks about the "fear of the Lord" very positively. Proverbs tells us,

> In the fear of the Lord there is strong confidence,
> And his children will have refuge.
> The fear of the Lord is a fountain of life,
> That one may avoid the snares of death. (Prov. 14:26–27 NASB)

Why? In Hebraic thought, the "fear of the Lord" (*yirat Adonai*[7]) is better understood as an awe and reverence for God that causes us to want to do his will. The "fear of the Lord" in these passages is an awe-filled love of God that allows us to grow in deeper knowledge of him. It teaches us how to live and reassures us of God's power and guidance. It gives us a reverence of his will that keeps us from getting caught in sins that will destroy our relationships and lives.

Rabbi Abraham Heschel points out that awe in response to God is far superior to fear. While fear focuses on one's self, awe focuses on God's glory. He writes:

> What is the nature of *yirah*? The word has two meanings, fear and awe. There is the man who fears the Lord lest he be punished in his body, family, or in his possessions. Another man fears the Lord because he is afraid of punishment in the life to come. Both types are considered inferior in Jewish tradition. . . . Fear is the anticipation and expectation of evil or pain, as contrasted with hope, which is the anticipation of good. Awe, on the other hand, is the sense of wonder and humility inspired by the sublime or felt in the presence of mystery. . . . Awe, unlike fear, does not make us shrink from the awe-inspiring object, but, on the contrary, draws us near to it. This is why awe is comparable to both love and joy.
>
> In a sense, awe is the antithesis of fear. To feel "The Lord is my light and my salvation" is to feel "Whom shall I fear?" (Ps. 27:1). "God is my refuge and my strength. A very present help in trouble. Therefore will we not fear, though the earth do change, and though the mountains be moved into the heart of the seas" (Ps. 46:2–3).[8]

Hebraically, the "fear of the Lord" is being aware of the awesome, holy presence of God. We see a reminder of this in many synagogues. Over the ornate cabinets that hold the Torah scrolls is the phrase *Know Before Whom You Stand*. We should realize that an infinitely powerful God is close at hand. Wow!

In worship, there really is no greater thrill than to feel spine-tingling awe at the grandeur of God. In this sense, to "fear" God is one of the most profound experiences of our lives, spiritually. We can see why the "fear of the Lord" as a sense of his presence is really the essence of a life of faith.

Double-Edged Words

The Hebrew word for "fear" can be either positive or negative, depending on the context. God's enemies fear him, but his people show him reverent, worshipful awe. Several other words show this same fascinating double-edged-ness too.

For instance, the word *pakad* can be a wonderful word or a terrible word, depending on where you find it. The King James Version translates it as "visit," but it has nothing to do with stopping by and saying hello. You've likely heard it used in Psalm 8:4: "What is man, that thou art mindful of him? and the son of man, that thou visitest him?" (KJV). Modern versions translate "visitest" here as "care for." We also encounter it in Ruth 1:6, where God "visited" his people by ending their famine. Later, in 1 Samuel 2:21, God "visited" Hannah by answering her tearful prayers for a son. Each time it means that God came to someone's aid or rescued them from a crisis.

It's a joyous thing when God "visits" us in the sense of caring for us and answering our prayers. But consider how *pakad* is used in Exodus 32:34: "In the day when I visit, I will visit their sin upon them." Here it has very negative implications. To "visit" a person's sins is to punish the person for them. In each of these lines, both positive and negative, *pakad* refers to the idea of "paying attention to." When God pays attention to a person, he cares for them. When he pays attention to someone's prayers, he answers them. But when he pays attention to someone's sins, he disciplines them.

Builder of the House

Remember our Emmaus road encounter and the puzzle of the word *Christ*? Knowing some of these multifaceted Hebrew meanings casts light on another mystery. God's messianic promise to David included another prophecy: that the Son of David would build a "house" for the Lord. Building the temple was the high point of Solomon's reign. Likewise, a key expectation of the Messiah was that he would build God's true temple. After all, God had declared, "He is the one who will build a house [*bayit*] for me, and I will establish his throne forever" (1 Chron. 17:12 NIV).

Often in Jesus' ministry he spoke about the temple, and he made a key statement that "I will destroy this temple made with hands, and in three days I will build another made without hands" (Mark 14:58 NASB). John's Gospel says that he was referring to his body, in terms of being raised to life. But there is a bigger picture there as well. Through Jesus' death and resurrection he was building a "house" of a different type. He was bringing together a "house" of a family of believers who would become that place where God's Spirit dwells.

Is it possible to equate a "house" as a temple with a "house" made of people? If you know Hebrew, it is. The word *bayit* can refer to a house, a temple, a family, or a lineage, among other things. In fact, God's prophecy to David pivoted on this very wordplay, which used two different meanings of *bayit*. King David had wanted to build God a "house," a temple, but God instead declared that he would build David a "house" in terms of a royal family lineage. Already we find a hint that the "house" Christ would build could be very different from the temples built by earlier kings.

At Pentecost, the Spirit indwelt the hearts of the believers. The people of the early church would have recalled other scenes of God's Spirit entering his temple, as it did in Solomon's day (2 Chron. 7:1–3). But now, instead of dwelling in houses made by human hands, the Spirit of God had moved into a new temple, the body of believers. This imagery is found throughout the New Testament:

> We are the temple of the living God. As God has said: "I will live with them and walk among them, and I will be their God, and they will be my people." (2 Cor. 6:16 NIV)

> Consequently, you are no longer foreigners and strangers, but fellow citizens with God's people and also members of his household, built on the foundation of the apostles and prophets, with Christ Jesus himself as the chief cornerstone. In him the whole building is joined together and rises to become a holy temple in the Lord. And in him you too are being built together to become a dwelling in which God lives by his Spirit. (Eph. 2:19–22 NIV)

> And coming to Him as to a living stone which has been rejected by men, but is choice and precious in the sight of God, you also, as living stones, are being built up as a spiritual house for a holy priesthood, to offer up spiritual sacrifices acceptable to God through Jesus Christ. (1 Pet. 2:4–5 NASB)

Now we can see a progression of God's plan to have intimacy with humankind, even though we forfeited our relationship with him through sin. When God first commanded Israel to build a tabernacle, the purpose was not just so he could dwell in it but could dwell *among them* (Exod. 29:45). Then he commissioned Solomon to build the temple and filled it with his presence. Finally, through the atoning work of Christ, God came to indwell our hearts as his *bayit*, his house, and achieve his greatest goal of living intimately with his people.

Vivid Imagery

Hebrew words often shed new light on difficult sayings in the Bible and can even challenge our theology. They also employ delightful imagery to illustrate their meaning, because few abstract words exist in the language. As a result, Hebrew is firmly rooted in the real world of the physical senses.

Without having the word *stubborn*, it uses "stiff-necked," evoking the image of an unwilling ox arching its neck to evade a yoke. Without having the word *stingy*, Hebrew speaks of being "tight-fisted" or of having a "bad eye"—being unable to see the needs of the person right in front of you.[9] Living without abstract terminology did not prevent the Bible's writers from expressing profound thoughts; it inspired them to paint colorful word pictures instead.

When Jacob's sons took advantage of a treaty to attack a Canaanite city, he chastised them by saying, "You have brought trouble on me by making me stink to the inhabitants of the land, the Canaanites and the Perizzites" (Gen. 34:30).

Hebrew speaks of being obnoxious or repulsive by speaking of a person's "bad odor," or *ba'ash* (bah-AHSH). You may recall how in Egypt, when Moses first came to Pharaoh to demand that he let his people go, Pharaoh increased Israel's workload instead. The elders of Israel confronted Moses by saying, "The LORD look on you and judge, because you have made us stink in the sight of Pharaoh and his servants, and have put a sword in their hand to kill us" (Exod. 5:21). The stench of the fish that died after the Nile turned to blood was nothing compared to how Israel "smelled" to the Egyptians!

Paul also used this graphic imagery when he told the Corinthians they were the "aroma" of Christ (the Messiah—the "*anointed one*") to those around them:

> But thanks be to God, who in Christ always leads us in triumphal procession, and through us spreads the fragrance of the knowledge of him everywhere. For we are the aroma of Christ to God among those who are being saved and among those who are perishing, to one a fragrance from death to death, to the other a fragrance from life to life. (2 Cor. 2:14–16)

Once again we find kingdom imagery, now of a "triumphal procession." After a war, the victors would lead their vanquished captives in a glorious parade through the streets and burn fragrant incense along the way. Paul was saying that to the lost we are the stench of death, but to those who are saved we are the life-giving fragrance of our richly anointed Messiah.

Paul was talking about a reality of life—you can conduct yourself in a Christlike way and still find yourself disliked, because others are convicted by your behavior. This analogy has another side, though. The way you "smell" is the aroma

Christ has to the world. If you're habitually rude or dishonest, it can be a potent witness *against* him. Whatever you do, don't be a stench!

A String around God's Finger

Sometimes Hebrew words can help us solve some biblical head-scratchers. For instance, in several places God says, "I will not remember your sins." But how can God, in his infinite intellect, forget something? And what does he expect of us, since we pray, "forgive us our sins as we forgive those who sin against us"? Does God really expect us to forgive and to forget the sins of others?

For some this is not just an academic question. A few years ago I heard a young woman recount nightmarish memories of being raped by a babysitter when she was ten. Over the years she had tried to forgive and sought healing. But as a Christian, she was plagued by the idea that God would not forgive her sins unless she forgave *and forgot* sins committed against her. How on earth could she ever forget?

Understanding the Hebrew words for "remember" and "forget" can help us untangle more than one theological knot. In English, our definition of the word *remember* focuses entirely on the idea of recalling memories and bringing ideas into our thoughts. To *forget* is to fail to bring a certain memory to mind. Both words are concerned entirely with mental activity—whether or not information is present. But the Hebrew verb *zakhar* has a much wider definition than just "remember." It includes both remembering and the actions that are taken because of remembering. It often implies that a person did a favor for someone, helped them, or was faithful to a promise or covenant. For instance:

> But God remembered Noah and all the beasts and all the cattle that were with him in the ark; and God caused a wind to pass over the earth, and the water subsided. (Gen. 8:1 NASB)

It sounds like God woke up one morning and slapped himself on the forehead, suddenly realizing that he'd left Noah bobbing around out on the waves. But the idea in this passage is that God acted upon his promise that Noah's family and the animals would be rescued from the flood.

Later in Genesis we find another example: "Then God remembered Rachel. He listened to her and opened her womb" (30:22 HCSB). Once again, the verb "remember" focuses on the action, not the mental activity. God paid attention to Rachel's needs, listened to her prayer, and answered it. Here, "remember" means "to intervene," focusing on what God *did*, not what God was thinking about.

The Idea of Forgetting

The Hebrew words for "forget," *shakach* and *nashah*, are also broad in scope. Often they mean to ignore, neglect, forsake, or disregard a person or covenant. For instance,

> So watch yourselves, that you do not forget the covenant of the LORD your God which He made with you, and make for yourselves a graven image in the form of anything against which the LORD your God has commanded you. (Deut. 4:23 NASB)

The idea here is that the Israelites would intentionally ignore their covenant, not necessarily forget that they made it. When the Israelites lapse into idolatry, we also hear God threatening to "forget" them:

> Therefore behold, I will surely forget you and cast you away from My presence, along with the city which I gave you and your fathers. (Jer. 23:39 NASB)

Once again the emphasis is on action rather than mental activity. God is saying that he would spurn his people, not lose their memory from his mind.

When God "forgets" something, he does not necessarily lack information. This helps us understand why, in the psalms, we hear people asking God why he is forgetting them:

> How long, O LORD? Will You forget me forever?
> How long will You hide Your face from me? (Ps. 13:1 NASB)

Here the psalmist is saying, "Why do you ignore my prayers and not intervene in my crisis?" God doesn't forget, but sometimes it seems as if he does.

Remembering Sins

Interestingly, *forget* is almost never used in combination with *sin*. But often the Bible does say that God will "not remember" our sins. The idea of "remembering sins" takes the idea of acting according to memory and puts it into a negative framework. It suggests that God is going to give the person what he or she deserves for the sin. He will punish sin, not just keep it on his mind. Consider:

> They have gone deep in depravity
> As in the days of Gibeah;
> He will remember their iniquity,
> He will punish their sins. (Hos. 9:9 NASB)

The second half of this verse contains a parallelism—meaning that it uses two phrases that are synonymous to emphasize an idea. To "remember their iniquity" is the same as to "punish their sin." It is automatically negative, implying that God will intervene to bring justice. So, to *not* remember sins is to decide not to punish them.

> If a wicked man restores a pledge [and] pays back what he has taken by robbery . . . he shall surely live; he shall not die. None of his sins that he has committed will be remembered against him. (Ezek. 33:15–16 NASB)

Because Hebrew focuses on the action rather than the thought, it doesn't necessarily imply that God loses the memory of sins in his infinite mind. It simply means that he has decided to forgo prosecution.

Knowing that Hebrew often focuses on actions rather than mental states, we can now see how God can "forget" people yet not forget. Or how he can choose not to "remember" sins yet not erase them from his memory. God chooses to put them aside, to ignore them and not bring them up again.

If you've ever been in a close relationship, you know what this is like. A wife whose feelings are hurt by her husband (or vice versa) "decides to forget"—to put the offense out of her mind even though the memory doesn't go away. Out of love, you simply choose not to act in revenge for the sin. And once you have done this, the memory itself tends to subside.

So what do we do with not being able to forget the sins of others, like the woman who couldn't forget her attacker? Have we really forgiven them? I find it helpful to consider that the Hebraic idea of "remembering sins" really encompasses the idea of *seeking revenge* for sins, not just knowing about them.

I find this very freeing in terms of understanding God's expectations of us. Often we struggle with a person who has hurt us repeatedly and wonder whether forgiveness means to pretend that the person won't act the same way again. Are we allowed to protect ourselves, even if we hope they'll change? The idea that we can decide not to "remember" someone's sins in terms of seeking revenge allows us to remember in order to make a situation better and make wise decisions in the future.

You know, if God could simply delete things from his data banks, he would have a much easier job than humans, who can't erase their memories. When we forgive a person, we need to choose to put aside our grievances, and often we need to do that over and over again as the memory returns to our minds.

When you think about it, it shows more love to be hurt and choose to not remember, time and time again, rather than to simply be able to forget about an incident. But interestingly, the more we love one another, the easier it becomes to remove the memory of the past from our minds. In this sense, perhaps God's infinite love really does entirely remove our sins from his infinite mind.

Becoming a "Collector" of Hebrew Words

What can you do to study the Bible with an awareness of these rich Hebrew words? It might sound like you need to learn a whole new language, but that's not actually true. The very first word of Hebrew I learned started unlocking doors of insight into the Bible, and each one after that cracked open yet others I had never thought to knock on before. After a while I started noticing interesting wordplays and humorous imagery, as my ears began tuning in to the Bible speaking in its own native language.

If you are passionate and reasonably intelligent, the best possible way to do this is to take Hebrew (and Greek) classes to learn to read the Bible in its original languages. But if you just can't take the time, or you're in the process but really want to start studying the words, you can at least get started during your Bible study time. Start making a mental list of interesting words and become familiar with them through your personal encounter with them in God's Word, not just by getting a definition out of a dictionary. Start with just a few and meditate on them in their biblical setting, in the passages where they occur. Encounter them alive in the biblical text, first in one scene, then in another. At the end of this book is a list of thirty fascinating Hebrew words to get you started, along with some tips and resources to keep learning.

Knowing more about the Hebrew way of looking at the world is helpful in reading the Scriptures from beginning to end. You'll see humor, irony, and timeless wisdom where you passed it by before. And often knowing the original, fuller sense of a biblical idea will challenge and change you when its ancient wisdom puts your life into the perspective of God's eternal Word.

TOOLS AND REFLECTIONS

Reading

1. Read about the Great Commandment in Mark 12:28–31. Then look up the wider definitions of *hear*, *love*, *heart*, *soul*, and *law* in appendix B, "Thirty Useful Hebrew Words for Bible Study." How does knowing more about the meaning of each word expand your understanding of this important passage? (For more, see chapters 2–4 of my book *Walking in the Dust of Rabbi Jesus*.)

2. Read through appendix B. Look up some of the verse references in a couple of different Bibles, or compare them at an online Bible study website like BibleGateway.com or BlueLetterBible.com.

3. In a group, ask if any members speak more than one language or grew up in a family that did. Do they know of any words that simply have no English equivalent or have a different connotation than their English equivalent?

Thoughts for Going Deeper

- I wrote a short ebook to supplement this chapter called *5 Hebrew Words That Every Christian Should Know*. The book explores five fascinating Hebraic words in the Scriptures. It includes links to three translations at

BibleGateway.com so that readers can see the variety of ways each word is translated. If you have time, check it out. (Available at OurRabbiJesus.com or on Amazon Kindle.)

- Check out my book *Listening to the Language of the Bible: Hearing It through Jesus' Ears* (Tverberg and Okkema, En-Gedi, 2004), which is a devotional guide to sixty-one Hebrew words and cultural ideas. A companion Bible study is also available for digging deeper.
- The *Cultural Backgrounds NIV Study Bible* (Walton and Keener, Zondervan, 2016) also has a very nice list of about fifty Hebrew words and verse references for looking them up. See pages xix–xxvi.
- If you want to study Hebrew or Greek yourself, I highly recommend the courses from the Biblical Language Center (BiblicalLanguageCenter.com).

PART 2

How the Bible Thinks

Big Picture Ideas That You Need to Understand

5

* * *

Greek Brain, Hebrew Brain

Cows, Creeds, and Concrete Metaphors

What does a nerdy teenager think about in church when the sermon has lost its glow? When I was fourteen, I'd mentally challenge myself to recall the titles of every *Star Trek* episode (the original series, of course). I had nothing on Galileo, though. When he got bored in church he would conduct scientific experiments right from his pew.

One day when he was seventeen he started observing the swinging of the chandelier that hung in the cathedral of Pisa. Sometimes it swayed slowly and leisurely around its resting point, but then the wind would catch it and send it sailing quickly to and fro over a wider arc. By counting his heartbeats, Galileo timed how long the chandelier took to swing one full cycle. The number of heartbeats he counted never changed, whether the width of the swing was large or small. This is how he discovered the law of *isochronism*: that the period (the time of one full cycle) of a pendulum is a constant. This would allow later inventors to construct clocks that kept constant time whether the pendulum swung fast or slow. While everyone else took sermon notes, Galileo was working out fundamental laws of physics.[1]

Even though I live four hundred years after Galileo, we are both part of the Western cultural world that embraces an analytical approach to life. Galileo lived at the beginning of modern science, and I dreamed that if I lived long enough, science would allow me to beam aboard the starship *Enterprise* someday. In college I majored in physics, and later I got my PhD in biology. More than most people, I appreciate the power of scientific analysis.

What Galileo and I learned to do was to sift through all the messiness of reality to find clean, simple, abstract truths. This habit grew out of a "new" style of thinking that actually began back in ancient Greece in the fifth century BC. European-based cultures of the Western world have been deeply influenced by it since the Enlightenment.

The Greeks' analytical approach has created an enormous gulf between the biblical world and ours. The gap is widest between us and the Old Testament, but even the New Testament often speaks with an old world accent. Israel was not untouched by Hellenism, but the Judaism of Jesus' day retained much of its traditional, Hebraic, Middle Eastern pattern of thought.

Jesus' style of communicating through parables and concrete images reflects the ancient, time-honored traditional method of communicating truth in his world. Paul communicated to his Greek-speaking audience in a more Western style, using propositions and logic. Modern readers find his writing much more readable. That was Paul's mission, of course—to take the gospel to the Gentiles and help it make sense to their way of thinking.

What many people don't realize is that even in Paul's writings, Hebraic thought patterns lurk just below the surface. He needed a foot in both worlds to communicate from the one to the other. Getting a sense for the Bible's ancient Hebraic style of thinking is a critical key for unlocking the text as a whole.

The Greeks' Great Idea

It seems remarkable that twenty-five hundred years after the Greek philosophers lived, our culture remains deeply influenced by their ideas. But what occurred there was not just a cultural shift but rather a radical innovation in thinking itself. You might call it "Thinking 2.0." It was a slick new programming language that made "if-then" reasoning quick and easy.

Greek philosophers realized the amazing power of converting their experience into simple, abstract ideas that they could manipulate mentally. For example, Galileo observed many chandeliers and then distilled from his data a simple, universal law that would allow him to predict what any pendulum would do in the future.

Plato put it something like this: in the room where you're reading this book, you likely have a table, which is made out of a particular material and has a certain height and length.

It's different from almost every other table yet shares characteristics with all of them. Rather than thinking about this one particular table, Plato said, "Why don't we just think about a table in the abstract?" The concept of "tableness" is simple and pure and applies to all tables everywhere. It will also outlive the table in your room, which will eventually get wobbly, break a leg, and one day be thrown out.

More practically, once you enter into Plato's abstract world, you can dissect your imaginary table into more precise concepts about particular attributes of tables, like "woodenness," "durability," "beauty," or "rectangularity." You can contemplate heady ideas like "materiality" or even "existence." Once you shift into a world of abstract ideas, you can explore it in infinitely more detailed ways than when you only think in terms of concrete, particular, real-world things.

This habit of abstracting and analyzing soon proved to be useful for all sorts of other things. Amazing truths could be found by studying, splitting, categorizing, and simplifying reality into concepts that could be mentally manipulated. Math, astronomy, and geometry were just the beginning, but what amazing power lay within them! Points, lines, and angles could be constructed into a marvelous universe of shapes and forms.

Greek philosophers also discovered that they could build elegant arguments by boiling down ideas into simple abstractions, which they carefully linked together according to the rules of formal logic. For example:

All men are mortal.

Socrates is a man.

Therefore Socrates is mortal.

Or

I think, therefore, I am.[2]

The Greeks loved to debate, and this technique of linking together "therefores" allowed them to construct convincing proofs quickly, as well as to demolish an opponent's argument by dissecting and analyzing it for contradictions. You don't need to spend as much time analyzing whether what a person says describes reality when you can reduce it to abstract categories and then reject or accept it based on its internal logic.[3]

The Greek culture was intoxicated by the power of this new "hyper-rational" way of thinking, and it spread to every land that Alexander the Great conquered, along with the rest of the Greek worldview. As a result, the Greeks' cultural descendants in the Western world have made their style of reasoning central to how we think and communicate. Down through the ages, this powerful method of analysis has led to enormous intellectual breakthroughs and fueled an explosion of the sciences.[4]

Our Condescending Attitude

If you're an educated Westerner, you're very accustomed to Thinking 2.0. You might assume that intelligent thought is impossible without it. But much of the Bible, especially the Old Testament, reflects an ancient form of reasoning and communication that actually worked quite well before Thinking 2.0 came along.

It was difficult for the ancient Greeks to imagine that anyone could even think rationally if they didn't use their Thinking

2.0 system of logical deduction. To the Greeks, the only thing that could come out of foreigners' mouths was "*bar*, *bar*, *bar*," like the bleating of a sheep, giving rise to the tradition of labeling non-Greeks as "barbarians."

If you live in Western culture, this condescending attitude has likely rubbed off on you. What sounds educated and sophisticated to us is the ability to convince through abstract reasoning. To communicate an important idea, we'll link together a lengthy set of arguments into a logical proof. We don't see a person as worthy of intellectual respect otherwise. New Testament professor Gary Burge observes,

> Our culture is a master of droning prose. We believe that religious speakers are effective when they can string out long arguments to defend their points, when they can persuade by the force of argument—this for us is theological sophistication. But this view betrays an important Western prejudice, that storytelling cultures are less sophisticated than prose cultures like our own. They are not![5]

Scholar Kenneth Bailey confesses that this attitude caused him to disrespect Jesus as an intellectual for many years. When he first began as a New Testament professor, his academic training in philosophy and systematic theology made him greatly admire Paul's arguments. Jesus' storytelling approach, however, did not impress him. Even though Bailey worshiped Christ as the Son of God and Savior of the world, it seemed like he was simply spinning moral tales for villagers and fisherfolk.

It was only after spending decades in the Middle East that Bailey rethought his disdainful estimation of Jesus. He realized that Jesus was communicating in a very sophisticated way, but in the style of his Mediterranean world, not of the West. Jesus was engaging at a high level with scholars of his day. Bailey realized that Jesus, rather than Paul, was the major theologian of the New Testament.[6]

Concept versus Illustration

Bailey explains that Westerners do their serious thinking and communication in *concepts*. We might include a story or illustration to simplify an idea or to make it memorable, but to us, the concept is always primary, not the illustration. Middle Easterners, in contrast, often use parables, metaphors, and proverbs as sophisticated forms of communication. "In the Middle East, from the beggar to the king, the *primary* method of creating meaning is through the creative use of metaphor and story," Bailey writes.[7]

What does this look like? When John the Baptist confronted the religious leaders, he didn't lecture them about the flaws in their theology by saying,

> Your externalized, merit-based observance assumes a soteriology based on ethnocentric nationalism that will ultimately prove erroneous and ineffective.

Rather, he bellowed:

> You brood of vipers! Who warned you to flee from the coming wrath? Produce fruit in keeping with repentance. And do not begin to say to yourselves, "We have Abraham as our father." For I tell you that out of these stones God can raise up children for Abraham. The ax is already at the root of

> the trees, and every tree that does not produce good fruit will be cut down and thrown into the fire. (Luke 3:7–9 NIV)

John vented his fury at the religious leaders with vigorous, concrete, real-world images. They were slithering snakes, fruitless deadwood that needed to be pruned out and burned. John employed punchy, vivid realities from the physical world to drive home his rebuke. This passionate, picturesque style has been characteristic of the Middle East from biblical times until today.

The Pen Is Mightier Than the Sword

What do languages do when they don't have many abstractions? You might assume that a technical vocabulary is necessary to express complex ideas. But consider this line from the book of Ecclesiastes:

> Again I saw under the sun that the race is not to the swift, or the battle to the strong, or bread to the wise, or riches to the discerning, or favor to the skillful; rather, time and chance happen to all of them. (Eccles. 9:11 HCSB)

A Westerner might express the same idea in these words:

> Objective considerations of contemporary phenomena compel the conclusion that success or failure in competitive activities exhibits no tendency to be commensurate with innate capacity, but that a considerable element of the unpredictable must invariably be taken into account.[8]

Hebrew expresses profound thoughts by telescoping ideas down into simple, concrete images. "Under the sun," of course, describes everything in the experience of human life. "Bread" refers to all food, the "battle" refers to military aggression and warfare. Here, the language is employing *metonyms*—concrete nouns that represent a broader category. We do the same in English when we speak of the "White House" to refer to the US government or say "the pen is mightier than the sword."

Indeed, "the pen is mightier than the sword" would fit in well in a Hebraic culture, where sophisticated ideas are expressed as proverbs constructed out of concrete images. You could convert it to abstractions if you want, which would sound much more intellectual and persuasive to a Western audience: "Journalistic advocacy is a more effective actuator of societal transformation than armed confrontation." But as long as you know what each metonym stands for, it makes just as much sense expressed concretely.

Notice, though, that you can't evaluate a proverb by its internal logic. You can't refute this line by saying, "No, that is impossible. Pens are not mightier than swords." The truth of this saying doesn't come from how flawlessly it has linked together "therefores." It comes from the fact that it describes a reality, albeit a surprising one—that a well-crafted newspaper article can do more to change the world than a military battle.

The Power of Concrete Metaphor

Jesus' stories were not just vague metaphors, Rorschach blots to be interpreted whatever way the listener chose. Often he spelled out the overall concept he was teaching before or after he told a parable. His illustrations were not just funny, feel-good stories for the kids. The depth and subtlety of his imagery should spur our most profound thinking.

Jesus' pictorial, concrete communication style carried on in the tradition of the Hebrew Scriptures that he read. For instance, look at Isaiah 53:7:

> He was oppressed and afflicted,
> yet he did not open his mouth;
> he was led like a lamb to the slaughter,
> and as a sheep before its shearers is silent,
> so he did not open his mouth. (NIV)

Here, Isaiah is sharing both an illustration and a concept. The *concept* is that God's Servant will suffer injustice. The *illustration*, about the Servant being like a lamb led to slaughter, is actually far more important. It's not just a poetic description of affliction that has been added for color.

The evocative imagery of a lamb silently submitting to its killers provokes us to meditate on the emotional impact. Why is the lamb helpless? Why does it not resist at this critical moment? Down through the ages, generations have pondered the implications.

This scene in Isaiah also expects its hearers to recall echoes of rich imagery woven through the Scriptures—the temple sacrifices, the Passover lamb, and Abraham's words to Isaac that "God will provide for himself the lamb" (Gen. 22:8). Likewise, the parabolic words of Jesus are pregnant, heavy-laden with imagery from the Scriptures, evoking memories of scenes from Israel's past and God's promises for the future.

Our Western instinct is to boil a story down to a concept. But when we do this with Isaiah 53:7, we lose the depth and complexity of the multilayered imagery. The Jewish authors of the New Testament realized this. Over and over they spoke of Christ as the "Lamb who was slain," referring to the entire scene in Isaiah rather than reducing it to a theological label (see Acts 8:32; 1 Cor. 5:7; 1 Pet. 1:19; Rev. 5:6, 12).

Part of the strength of concrete metaphors is that they convey emotion. That's actually why Western intellectual arguments avoid them, though. The goal of a logical proof is to convince hearers through facts and reason alone, without appealing to emotions. The Greeks valued *detachment*, subduing emotions so that intellect could reign supreme. But Middle Easterners believed it was just as important to convey the emotional component of their ideas.

Love in the Abstract?

Gradually, the Greeks built a whole new vocabulary to describe the theoretical notions that fascinated them.[9] English and other European languages are similarly equipped with high-powered abstract nouns like *epistemology*, *globalization*, and *omnipotence*. These terms have the advantage of being unambiguous and precise. Complex ideas can be compressed into single words. Many indigenous languages are like biblical Hebrew, however, in which abstractions are rare.

Believe it or not, the Old Testament is usually much easier to translate than the New, because its concrete language makes more sense to the non-Western world. The Greek language's propensity for abstraction often makes translating the New Testament quite difficult.

Bible translator Dave Brunn points out even the simple word *love* can create problems.[10] In English and Greek, we're used to talking about love as an abstraction, without anyone actually doing it. But in the New Guinean language he studies, love is *always* a verb, an action between two people. God loves you. You love your neighbor. *Love* can't be used in a sentence without specifying who is doing the loving and who is being loved. In the Hebrew Bible, *love* can be a noun but it is always attached to a person: "God's love" or "the love of Jacob for Rachel."[11] Love is never spoken of as an abstract idea on its own.

For Brunn, translating Paul's famous line that "Love is patient, love is kind . . ." (1 Cor. 13:4 NIV) was a head-scratcher, because Paul doesn't say who is loving whom. Paul was doing a very Greek thing by talking about the *idea* of love, all by itself. In order to render this line so that the New Guineans might understand it, Brunn needed to convert "love" back into a verb and supply a *lover* and a *beloved*, translating it as, "The person who loves people acts patiently towards other people."

We are spoiled in the West by our tradition of focusing on love as an abstract concept. What we're doing is using Plato's trick to formulate a mental idea of "love" that can be dissected, analyzed, and detached from reality. This detached attitude allows us to ignore the actual *doing* of the thing we talk about, feeling quite superior in having lofty thoughts about it instead.

Notice, though, that there's nothing wrong with the Greek habit of speaking in abstractions. It's merely a different way of communicating. What's important is that we become *translators* between these two ways of thinking. Paul's words about love may have been expressed in the abstract, but if they transform us into people who are patient and kind to others, they've hit home and entered our concrete reality too.

Formed from Mere Dust

Instead of employing abstractions, Hebrew expects listeners to infer meaning from its concrete imagery. If you're not aware of this, you can easily gloss right past some of its most profound statements. For instance, when Westerners read Genesis 2:7, "The LORD God formed a man from the dust of the ground and breathed into his nostrils the breath of life" (NIV), they often focus only on the physical details. In contrast, Jewish scholar Nahum Sarna interprets Genesis 2:7 in a more Hebraic way, being sensitive to the meaning of the concrete imagery within the ancient world:

> [This] image simultaneously expresses both the glory and the insignificance of man. Man occupies a special place in the hierarchy of Creation and enjoys a unique relationship with God by virtue of his being the work of God's own hands and being directly animated by God's own breath. At the same time, he is but dust taken from the earth, mere clay in the hands of the divine Potter, who exercises absolute mastery over His Creation.[12]

Sarna understands this line as being a paradoxical statement about our unique value within God's creation, that we draw our lives from God himself but are formed from nothing but dirt. Throughout the Bible, "dust" signified insignificance or finiteness. When Abraham spoke to God, he humbly declared that he was "but dust and ashes" (Gen. 18:27). God "raises the poor from the dust and lifts the needy from the ash heap" (Ps. 113:7), but he "tramples kings underfoot; he makes them like dust with his sword, like driven stubble with his bow" (Isa. 41:2). When you read the Old Testament, it's important not to underestimate the amount of meaning that the physical imagery is trying to convey.

Western readers assume that if a text is historical, it will include physical details only to record the setting. If it contains symbolism, we assume it must be legendary. Eastern historical accounts, however, will often pick and choose among factual details for imagery that conveys meaning in concrete ways. The Bible narrative (especially the Old Testament) is typically quite succinct, and when it goes into descriptive detail, it's often for a reason.

For instance, consider King Saul, Israel's first king. You might expect a detailed analysis of his personality flaws that ultimately cost him his kingship. Instead, this information is communicated in concrete ways by choice of the scenes we see him in. When Saul finds out he's to be anointed as king, he has been wandering for days looking for some lost donkeys (1 Sam. 9:5–10). When he's later announced, he's hiding behind some baggage (10:22). The physical details surrounding these events highlight Saul's inadequacy and ill-preparation for the task of kingship. Much of his biography is not recorded, but a few selected scenes are chosen for what they say about him more broadly.[13]

The Way Parables Worked

Jesus' parables fit perfectly into this culture that expressed itself through specific, tangible metaphors. He was engaging in sophisticated theological teaching, but we miss it if we are looking for the deductive abstract arguments of the Greeks. Jesus often based his reasoning on *experience* rather than if-then logic. He did this in multiple ways.

Experience of the Natural World

Jesus frequently used observations about nature and daily life to shed light on spiritual realities. Sometimes he highlighted a lesson by pointing out what was obviously true: grapes don't grow on thornbushes. Likewise, people are known by their "fruit." That seems pretty logical.

More often, however, Jesus used physical examples that have a surprising *illogic* about them to shed light on the mysterious ways of God. A tiny mustard seed can grow into an enormous tree. A blossom that wilts in a day is more gorgeously adorned than a king's robe. Tiny clues from creation give us a glimpse into God's unfathomable ways.

In contrast, Western reasoning often attempts to systematize theology by reducing and affixing God's thoughts onto a logical grid, flattening and straightening them so that they fit into predictable patterns. Jesus' parables, however, embraced the fact that our material world is multifaceted and complex. If God's creation surprises and perplexes us, shouldn't its Creator do so even more?

Experience of Human Behavior

Jesus often used examples based on human experience to explain the complexity of God's ways. A farmer finds tares growing in his wheat fields. Wouldn't the logical response be to pull them out? Knowing that the valuable wheat crop would be damaged in the process, the farmer instead decides to let the tares grow. In the same way, God allows evildoers to live alongside the righteous.

Jesus was doing theology through storytelling. He was addressing a conundrum that has perplexed philosophers down through the ages: How can a good God let evil seemingly go unchecked? Jesus' answer was to share a parallel situation, an experience where a human farmer would make that decision. God knows the wider situation and, for the ultimate good, puts off judgment until the end. What seems illogical at first is not, in God's greater wisdom.

Experience of the Scriptures

Parables often use imagery from the Scriptures, which recounted the history of Israel's experience with God. Certain memorable motifs came up over and over again. Kings, wedding banquets, shepherds searching for sheep, and farmers at harvest are all images that appear in Jesus' parables and in those of other rabbis. Both the plots and the punch lines could allude to scenes in the Bible. If it was true before, it could be true again.

Take, for instance, the fruit tree with an axe at its roots that John the Baptist used in his rebuke in Luke 3. He took this motif from the prophets, who often used trees to represent a nation or its leaders. God might let them flourish or grow imposingly tall. But in a moment they could be chopped down or consumed in a fire (see Jer. 11:16; 24:1–10; Ezek. 15:6; 17:22; 20:47, 31; Dan. 4:14). Often Israel is the tree, and the image is of God's judgment of the nation.

We find a similar tree in one of Jesus' parables. A man owns an unfruitful tree that he wants to chop down. The gardener, however, buys the tree one more year of life by promising to tend and fertilize it (Luke 13:6–8). When you compare the two stories, you can see the difference between Jesus' theological viewpoint and John the Baptist's. Both are talking about the timing of God's judgment. Is it right around the corner, or might it be delayed? John is convinced that the end is close at hand. Jesus disagrees but preaches that now is the time to repent. Both are using metonyms from the Bible to preach eschatology, where "trees" are nations and "axes" are God's judgment.

What's interesting is that one place where such "axe" and "tree" imagery is especially prominent is the end of Isaiah 10:

> Behold, the Lord God of hosts
> will lop the boughs with terrifying power;
> the great in height will be hewn down,
> and the lofty will be brought low.
> He will cut down the thickets of the forest with an axe,
> and Lebanon will fall by the Majestic One.
> (vv. 33–34)

Immediately following this tree-chopping scene is the messianic prophecy of the "Branch":

> There shall come forth a shoot from the stump of Jesse,
> and a branch from his roots shall bear fruit. (11:1)

If you read these texts all as one, it sounds like the coming of the Messiah is the time of God's chopping of the trees.

This is likely why John and Jesus both used this metaphor. John's calling was to announce the coming of the messianic King and to reform his people's conduct in preparation for his arrival. John's ministry did just that, but he often spoke as if the Messiah himself would bring God's judgment.

While Jesus affirmed John's ministry, he challenged this idea, pointing out God's promises of coming with healing and forgiveness.[14] His parables often focused on God's mercy toward sinners and preached that judgment would be delayed until the end. For instance, Jesus likened the kingdom to a fishing net that catches both bad and good fish, which will be sorted later (Matt. 13:47–50). He also likened it to a weedy field that a farmer allows to keep growing to preserve the crop (vv. 25–40). Jesus did sophisticated theology in a very Hebraic way, using concrete, picturesque metaphors to prove his point.[15]

Learning from Galileo's Mistake

In one of the first labs I did in college, I learned a lesson from Galileo that impacted how I read the Bible today. In my physics lab, our experiment was to test Galileo's theory. Is the period of a pendulum a constant?

I smirked as my professor introduced the lab because I remembered hearing about Galileo's famous chandelier experiment in high school. Gleefully I began the experiment, feeling confident that while everyone else would expect that the period would change, I had secret knowledge that would allow me to ace my lab report.

My lab partner swung the ball from increasing angles and I ran the stopwatch. For the first several measurements, we had beautifully constant results. But farther out, the pendulum wouldn't *quite* make it back in time. My thumb started trying to help by anticipating its return. As the angles got larger and larger, I found myself fudging more and more to "help" the period be constant, as I knew it should be. When I turned in my report, with a lumpy graph and ill-behaved data, the grade I got reflected it. What a frustration.

A few weeks later we did the same lab, only now with a computer as timer, which aided in precision and eliminated my human input. This time the result was undeniable. At small angles, the period was a constant, but at larger angles it increased. When I plotted out the data, I got a smooth curve. For my lab report I looked up the research, and it turned out that Galileo's law of isochronism was only true if the angle was relatively small.[16]

Believe it or not, Galileo actually never gave up his theory. He tested it over and over with different equipment and insisted that measurements with flawed equipment could never prove it wrong. After all, his abstract theory was so mathematically beautiful and elegantly simple, it just *had* to be true, no matter what the results said. Only the abstract, ideal pendulum in his mind could tell him the truth, not the ones he actually saw before him.

Galileo's approach might sound reasonable if the last time you took science was in high school. There you did what you called "experiments," but the real "truth" came from the textbook. When your results didn't line up with the theory, you just declared your data wrong and chalked it up to experimental error.

When you walk into a real research laboratory, however, the situation is reversed. There, the data are where theories must *live* and *die*. I realized this when I began working on research for my PhD. Each experiment depended on the outcome of the last, and if I refused to believe my results, I'd be doomed. It was always tempting to hang on to a theory that seemed elegant and clever. But if the map and the ground do not agree, the map is wrong.

Later, when I worked with college students on research projects in my lab, each fresh-faced young person would start out by asking me, "What answer am I supposed to get?" My reply would be, "We don't know. That's why we call it research."

Greek-thinkers often fall into Galileo's trap—they tend to be so easily swayed by an elegant theological proof that they forget to check the biblical "data." We treat the Bible like Galileo did his pendulum data. When the numbers and the theory don't line up, we just go with the theory. Similarly, we often conduct our advanced discussions in the abstract rationalism of theology and don't check to see if the Bible actually confirms our ideas.

Here's an example. A while back a local newspaper ran a letter to the editor from a man who was sick and tired of Christians leaving witnessing tracts at his door. He concluded that if Jesus was alive today, he would likely tell Christians to stop evangelizing and just leave believers of other religions alone.

While I sympathize with this man's irritation at feeling targeted, it's another thing to make a statement about what Jesus would have thought of evangelism. What if we look in the New Testament? Throughout the Gospels Jesus sends out disciples two by two to preach the gospel. At Pentecost the first thing Peter does after being filled with the Spirit is preach to a large crowd of worshipers in the temple, and three thousand come to faith. And, of course, Paul travels far and wide to take the gospel to the Gentiles. If you're looking for evidence that Jesus would have seen evangelism as obnoxious, you simply won't find it. The whole New Testament records the history of the explosive growth of the church that was founded on Jesus' command to "make disciples of all nations" in Matthew 28:19.

Certainly, Christians can be obnoxious and manipulative in their evangelism efforts. We can ask how we can be more mature and Christlike in evangelism, but we can't rewrite theology with our own guesses based on the assumption that "Jesus must have taught it because it sounds more loving." If Jesus seems to be saying something obnoxious, could it be that it's our own worldview that needs reexamining?

I've heard this backward logic often recently. It usually takes a form something like this:

1. Christians are obnoxious when they say ________________________________.
2. But Jesus is love.
3. Therefore, he must not have said it.

This is a classic style of logic called a *syllogism*, which sounds wonderfully convincing to Greek-thinking brains. But what if we looked to the New Testament to ground our theology? After all, Jesus was a historical figure, not an abstraction.

Reading the Bible like a Berean

We have an example of a better approach with the Bereans. When Paul and Silas brought their amazing claims that Jesus was God's promised Messiah, the Bereans got out their Scriptures and did their research.

> Now these Jews were more noble than those in Thessalonica; they received the word with all eagerness, examining the Scriptures daily to see if these things were so. Many of them therefore believed, with not a few Greek women of high standing as well as men. (Acts 17:11–12)

If we know that God speaks through history, it offers an alternative to our usual way of answering theological questions. Often people pluck a line here and there from Jesus' words and then link it with a verse a dozen books away through a logical argument. We can easily concoct a whole new theology this way. If it sounds logical, Westerners will find it persuasive. But if the Bible speaks through history, we should check our theology in the wider record of the biblical text.

The book of Acts, I've found, is a great place to ground speculation about how Jesus' words were interpreted by his original disciples. The people there were believers who had heard Jesus firsthand. No time had elapsed for his words to be reinterpreted, and his followers were passionate about living them out. It's not unreasonable to conclude that what the early believers did (or at least tried to do) was what Jesus taught.

Let's try it out. Jesus preached about plucking out your eye or cutting off your hand if it causes you to sin (see Matt. 18:8–9 NASB). Did he mean this literally, or was it figurative, a bit of exaggeration for emphasis? Well, we find no reports of people actually plucking out their eyes in the rest of the New Testament. His audience obviously understood that Jesus was speaking figuratively here.

On the other hand, Jesus once told a wealthy man, "Go sell what you possess and give to the poor, and you will have treasure in heaven; and come, follow me" (Matt. 19:21). Were Jesus' teachings about extreme generosity just an exaggeration? Once again, look at Acts. There we find the early church selling their possessions and giving to the poor (Acts 4:32–35). This over-the-top response wasn't universal, but clearly, Jesus' strong words on generosity were taken quite seriously by his followers.

Here's another example. In my last book, *Walking in the Dust of Rabbi Jesus*, I quoted a radio program in which I heard a pastor say,

> When Jesus came, everything changed, everything changed. . . . He didn't just want to clean up the people's attitudes as they gave their sacrifices, He obliterated the sacrificial system because He brought an end to Judaism with all its ceremonies, all its rituals, all its sacrifices, all of its external trappings, the Temple, the Holy of Holies, all of it.[17]

Hmm . . . once again, how about looking at history? In the book of Acts, do we find the disciples abandoning the sacrificial system and the temple? After all, Jesus did denounce the corruption of the temple and prophesy its destruction, like other teachers of his day. Other groups actually did abandon temple worship, but the early disciples did quite the opposite. Peter and the other early believers participated daily in temple worship and even used the temple as their primary gathering place.

In Acts, do we find any evidence of Jesus' first disciples jumping for joy at being done with the law? Once again we find the opposite. Jewish believers in Jesus were careful to observe the Torah, and were known for their avid observance (Acts 21:20, 25). They even asked Paul to sponsor a sacrifice in order to show his commitment to living by the law (v. 24).

If Jesus intended to bring Jewish practice and the temple to an end, his followers certainly didn't catch his drift. Yet the church did rule in Acts 15 that Gentiles were not obligated to observe the laws given to the Jews on Mount Sinai. A growing number of scholars believe that the reason Christians haven't been obligated to observe the law is because they are Gentiles, not because Jesus abolished it. This would agree with his own declaration in Matthew 5:17.[18]

Instead of stringing together syllogisms in order to logically deduce what Christ *might* have meant, we can ask how his original audience attempted to live out his words. Certainly the broad sweep of Scripture is better grounding for our ideas than our habit of speculative theologizing. Often I find that reading Jesus' words in light of New Testament history challenges my preconceptions and refines my understanding of our calling as his disciples.

I Will Be Known by What I Do

Here we come to a more basic difference between Greek and Hebraic thought. The Greeks, like the rest of the ancient world, loved to speculate on the nature of the divine realm. In their early history, they invented elaborate myths to describe the battles and love affairs of their divine pantheon. When they discovered rationalism, they assumed that the same logic that allowed them to analyze physical reality should work to analyze the spiritual one. After all, they had been able to predict the movements of the stars and planets! Weren't the heavens the domain of the gods? Certainly they had stumbled onto the key to ultimate truth and even usurped the gods themselves.

The Hebrew attitude toward God was starkly different. You can see it when you compare the Scriptures of Israel to those of surrounding nations. All the polytheists had concocted elaborate mythologies and stories about their gods' origins, like the Greeks. The Scriptures of Israel contain no such tales. Genesis simply starts with the presumption that God exists, not bothering to prove his reality in any way. The creation account has no bloody battles to form the elements of the earth and sky, simply one mysterious Supreme Being who speaks creation into existence with a few majestic words.

When Moses asked this deity's name at the burning bush, God's strange response was: *eyeh asher eyeh*, which means "I am that I am," or "I will be what I will be" (see Exod. 3:14). Moses must have been stopped short by this remarkable reply. Pagan gods had names that likened them to heavenly objects, such as "sun" (*Shamash*) or "moon" (*Yarikh*), or to human rulers, such as "king" (*Molech*) or "exalted lord" (*Baal Zebul*). But this God's name was utterly unlike any other because this God was utterly beyond description. Just as his sanctuary was devoid of images or idols, his name also did not offer a likeness for comparison. This strange, superhuman entity that Israel had encountered was completely beyond human imagining.

Through God's name he was proclaiming how he would reveal himself: "*I will be known by what I do*." God didn't just flash lightning bolts from a thundercloud or define himself to Moses philosophically. Instead he redeemed his people from slavery, fed them manna daily, protected them from enemies, and delivered them to the promised land. He instructed them with his laws and rebuked them through the prophets.

This is why the Hebrew Bible doesn't actually contain much theological discussion. Rather it shows wide-screen, front-row footage of God's mighty acts in history. It records the visceral, moment-by-moment emotions of Israel's tempestuous relationship with God, from exaltation to despair and back again. Theologian Karl Barth puts it this way:

> No attempt is made in the Bible to define God—that is, to grasp God in our concepts. . . . The Bible tells the story of God; it narrates His deeds and the history of this God as it takes place on earth in the human sphere. The Bible proclaims the significance and the importance of this working and acting, this story of God, and in this way it proves God's existence, describes His being and His nature. The Bible is not a philosophical book, but a history book, the book of God's mighty acts, in which God becomes knowable to us.[19]

This is why the Old Testament is more comfortable with paradox and seeming contradiction than Western readers are. The Bible simply assumes that Israel had an unparalleled encounter with a being who was utterly outside human experience. It makes no attempt to explain or defend the strangeness of this mysterious entity. It merely describes Israel's powerful encounters with God through history.

A Creed with Cows in It?

With my scientific, analytical training, I grew up very much focused on seeing Christian faith as a set of beliefs. I had inherited the Greeks' love of ideas, so I saw religion as a list of doctrinal bullet points to be affirmed. But what if I removed my Greek spectacles? What would faith look like from a Hebraic perspective?

I discovered an important clue in the first class I ever took on Jesus' Jewish context. As the class began, my thoughts simmered on a stew of elementary questions about Judaism. What exactly did Jews believe, and how did it compare to Christianity? I wished that someone would spell it all out in a simple statement, a basic creed of some type.

Then one day my instructor started handing out copies of the *Shema* (pronounced "shmah"), a profession of faith that pious Jews have recited daily since before the first century. Eagerly, I scanned down the page of what I assumed was their Apostles' Creed.

I wasn't too surprised that it started off in a theological way, with God's command to love and worship him alone (Deut. 6:4–9).[20] But the next section, from Deuteronomy 11:13–21, stopped me in my tracks. I absolutely couldn't believe my eyes:

> I will send rain on your land in its season, both autumn and spring rains, so that you may gather in your grain, new wine and olive oil. I will provide grass in the fields for your cattle, and you will eat and be satisfied. (vv. 14–15 NIV)

Grain? New wine? Oil? I couldn't believe it. *Grass for cattle?* How could you get any less spiritual than cows? What on earth were barnyard animals doing in this central profession of faith? I was looking for spiritual truths, heady doctrines like the "communion of saints" and "forgiveness of sins." I sat there, stumped at the utter oddness of this choice of Scripture. Why on earth would this passage be so central?

Sometime later I learned why. The *Shema* isn't a list of core propositional statements to be affirmed. Rather, it is a daily recommitment to Israel's covenant with God. It begins with God's command to serve only him and then follows with other passages in Deuteronomy that recount God's promises to provide for their material needs.

I conceived of belief as mental assent to abstract statements of truth. My thinking was actually quite close to the gnostics, ancient heretics who misunderstood the gospel to say that what was essential to salvation was knowing certain spiritual truths, which would unlock the secret knowledge of the heavens.

The *Shema*, however, is a recollection of *history*, a reminder of the oath that established Israel's relationship with God. It doesn't list things to be believed. Yet it does assume that a person believes in the God whom they vow to love and serve. It contains beliefs but is actually far more than that. It is a recollection of the promise that the nation of Israel made centuries earlier on Mount Sinai. The words of the *Shema* are a binding reminder of the covenant that the Jewish people had committed themselves to on a smoky desert mountaintop centuries ago. This was what was critical to recount each day—the foundational event in Israel's history.

Wait, then. Why did I see a list of beliefs as the essence of my faith? There actually is a reason for their importance. The core command of the New Testament is to *believe in Christ* (John 20:31), and the Apostles' Creed is how the church has defined that. In early centuries the church was fraught with division and heresy, forcing it to expend great effort to establish clear boundaries and define exactly what it believed.

Theology is a wonderful tool for helping us understand the God who revealed himself in the Bible. But having your doctrinal ducks in a row is not what accomplishes salvation. If it were, wouldn't Satan be fully qualified?

What actually does the saving is Christ's atoning death for our sins. It's because of his sacrifice on the cross that we can have peace with God. What, then, would be a more Hebraic way to remind ourselves of this? How can we focus on this foundational event and ground ourselves in historical reality?

Believe it or not, Jesus himself gave us instructions. On his last evening with his disciples, he was celebrating Passover. This was an important religious feast, a covenantal meal that was a formal celebration of God's relationship with his people. It recounted the night God freed Israel from Egypt, reminded them of their current relationship, and recalled the promise of the Messiah, God's final redeemer. When Jesus broke bread and shared wine with his disciples, he told them to do this in remembrance of his coming death. Through his sacrifice, Christ was inaugurating the long-awaited "new covenant" for the forgiveness of sin that God had promised his people in Jeremiah 31.

As important as creeds are, what brings us into relationship with God is not a *creed* but the *covenant* Christ enacted that night. When you think about it, celebrating the Lord's Supper is very Hebraic and very non-Western. It is a tangible way to celebrate our relationship with God. We are sitting down to enjoy a meal together, an act that denotes intimate fellowship with God and all others at the table.[21] And we are actually, physically replaying the event in history that made possible our relationship with God through Christ.

TOOLS AND REFLECTIONS

Reading

1. Read Jesus' parable about the lilies of the field in Matthew 6:28–32. How is it based on our experience of the natural world?

2. Now, read Isaiah 40:6–8 and 40:21–24. How do you hear echoes of these passages in the lilies of the field parable? How does Jesus' inclusion of Scripture reinforce and affirm his teachings to his audience?

Thoughts for Going Deeper

- An outstanding resource is *Our Father Abraham: The Jewish Roots of the Christian Faith* by Marvin Wilson (Grand Rapids: Eerdmans, 1989). See especially the chapter "The Contour of Hebrew Thought," 135–65.
- Another excellent book that grapples with Hebraic, paradoxical thought is *The Gospel According to Moses: What My Jewish Friends Taught Me about Jesus* by Athol Dickson (Grand Rapids: Brazos Press, 2003).
- Also helpful would be the chapters "Thinking with Both Hands" and "The Secrets That God Keeps" in my book *Walking in the Dust of Rabbi Jesus*, 130–41, 154–64.

6

Why Jesus Needs Those Boring "Begats"

Knowing the Family Rules

Bible translators tell some shocking stories. In my Hebrew class in Israel, I met a translator who had come to brush up on his language skills for his work in the Philippines. One day he shared an experience that was quite telling. According to him, the preliminary version of Matthew that translators made for one language group in the Philippines had left out the "begats." Missionaries wanted to share the gospel as quickly as possible, so translators hadn't included the genealogical list, not thinking it was important. It seemed silly to them to begin with a distracting, irrelevant list of names.

When the complete New Testament translation was released, more than one person asked, "Do you mean that

Jesus was a real person?" The first readers had assumed that the Gospels were fables told about a magical, fictional hero. In their way of thinking, without a family line Jesus didn't even exist. Ancestry was as critical to them as it was to the Bible's writers. In many cultures in the world, a family line is essential to have any identity at all.

In our Western world, a brand-new Christian might expect to open the Bible to a book of moral lessons or philosophy. Instead, we find a long and winding epic of a family that God has chosen. You may be surprised at how many biblical subplots expect the reader to be aware of the Bible's family-centered logic and the assumptions surrounding it. Not only is family central in the Old Testament but it is key to some very important controversies in the New Testament as well, such as including Gentiles among the growing movement of Jewish believers in Jesus. Grasping the ideas that ancient peoples had about the family and how these themes play out can help us understand our Bibles from beginning to end.

The church where I grew up had little interest in the Old Testament, especially the "begats," which seemed to be just a fat, outdated phone book. It would also bother us that biblical families weren't always Ward and June Cleaver. However, you don't have to assume that the polygamy and concubinage of the ancient world are a model for us today to grasp how the biblical world "thought." You may find ancient practices unsavory, but they are based in cultural attitudes that form the framework of Scripture's story of redemption. Until you grasp how family relationships framed life as the ancient world understood it, you won't get the point of many major biblical themes.

Over the history of the world, most people have understood the biblical emphasis on family much more than we do today. Family was the framework upon which society was built. Traditional cultures throughout history have structured themselves in terms of extended family relationships. As Western individualists, however, we find it difficult to appreciate this prominent theme in the Bible that would have been obvious to its original audience.

Like Father, Like Son

The Hebrew word for "son," *ben*, is used for many purposes in the Bible, and it carries certain cultural assumptions. Along with its literal meaning, the word often refers to later descendants as well. This is why, in genealogies, generations can be left out and only significant ancestors reported. This is not an error—it was normal to speak of a later descendant as a "son."

In the ancient Near East, a common expectation was that sons would take on their father's profession and serve the same god or gods that he did. Along with this inherited identity came a strong assumption that children would resemble their father in personality too. If a father was wise, his descendants would be wise; if he was warlike, his descendants would be warlike. The apple would not fall far from the tree. When Jesus is described as the "Son of David," it tells us that he is a descendant in the line of David, and like David he is a powerful king.

You can hear Jesus using this same logic in his preaching about being "sons of your Father."

> Love your enemies and pray for those who persecute you, so that you may be sons of your Father who is in heaven. For he makes his sun rise on the evil and on the good, and sends rain on the just and on the unjust. (Matt. 5:44–45)

Our Father graciously sustains both the good and the evil with sunshine and rain. Of course, as his children, we aim to emulate him. We are carrying on our family tradition of loving-kindness when we aim to do good even to those who persecute us.

Family Memories

Memory, history, and family were central to the fabric of the biblical world, and we need to read the Bible with these in mind. Explaining what each family was like and the relationships between families was very important to understanding the society as a whole. Stories about the founders of each family were key to each family's self-definition.

I used to read the book of Ruth as just a story of a woman who snagged a good husband because she was kind to her mother-in-law. I couldn't really appreciate it until I learned about Ruth's family history and how it fit into the longer "soap opera" of the narrative.

In biblical times, our ears would have pricked up at the scandalous fact that Ruth was a *Moabite*. We would recall that when the weary Israelites were journeying to the promised land, the people of Moab lured them into sexual immorality and idol worship (Num. 25:1). Then we'd recall their origins in Genesis 19:30–38, in the not-so-nice story of Lot and his daughters. After escaping the destruction of Sodom and Gomorrah, they got their father drunk so that they could become pregnant by him, since their husbands had refused to leave the city and had died. One gave birth to a son named Moab, and he became the father of the Moabite people. In ancient thinking, this made sense. If your ancestors were immoral, you'd likely be the same way too.

Look at the story of Ruth with this in mind. Not only was Ruth a Moabite but she was even in the same situation as Lot's daughters: a widow who desperately needed children. Naomi even told her to approach Boaz when he was sleeping outside by his harvest, after he had eaten (and drunk) his fill. But Boaz proclaimed that, unlike her ancestors, she was a virtuous woman (Ruth 3:10). Then he married her, and her son became the grandfather of King David. Not only that, but Ruth even appears in Matthew 1:5 as part of the line of Christ!

To an ancient reader, it would have been shocking that not only did the God of Israel accept Ruth and cleanse her from her family history but he also gave her a key role in his supreme act of salvation. Those of us who struggle with an embarrassing family history or an immoral past should rejoice to see how God redeemed Ruth and used her for his wonderful purposes.

Your Family Is Your Identity

Think back to the last time you introduced yourself. After sharing your name, one of the first things you were likely asked is, "So, what do you do?" You'd label yourself in terms of your job title and place of work, and maybe mention your education and where you live. For many people, your job is a big part of your self-identity. Sometimes it seems to be everything. Do you remember the beginning of *Jeopardy!* the game show? Each contestant is introduced by a booming voice from above as a spotlight illuminates him or her. Then we hear:

> A currency trader from Chicago, Illinois . . .
>
> A library circulation clerk from Dallas, Texas . . .
>
> A tax accountant from Portland, Oregon . . .

Each person is boiled down to two things: what they do and where they live.

Now, contrast this to how an indigenous person from Somalia would introduce himself, as author Ryszard Kapuscinski describes in his book *The Shadow of the Sun*:

> The Somali is born somewhere on the road, in a shack-tent or directly under the open sky. . . . He has but a single identity—it is determined by his ties to family, to the kinship group, to the clan. When two strangers meet, they start by asking, "Who are you?" "I am Soba," the first one begins, "from the family of Ahmad Abdullah, which belongs to the Mussa Arraye group, which is from the clan of Hasean Said, which is part of the larger Isaaq clan," etc. After this, the second stranger gives the particulars of his lineage, his roots. The exchange lasts a long time and is immensely important, because both individuals are trying to determine whether something unites them or divides them, whether they should embrace or attack each other with knives. Their personal rapport, their mutual sympathy or antipathy, have no meaning; their relationship, be it friendly or hostile, depends on the current

> state of affairs between their two clans. The human being, the singular, distinct person, does not exist—or he matters only as part of this or that bloodline.[1]

Soba's reality, where a person defines him- or herself through family identity, seems nearly unimaginable to us. We think in terms of our individual tastes and achievements, not in terms of our genealogical tree. But before our industrial age, families and clans defined the world, not businesses or, believe it or not, individuals.

Consider the fact that in the ancient world, people regularly experienced infant mortality and witnessed death by accident, disease, and warfare. What was enduring was not so much the individual but the family, and people thoroughly invested themselves in the larger identity of their family.

Look at what the metaphor of a family as a "tree" tells us. Each individual is like a twig that will leaf out and bear fruit, but at some point it will wither and die. The tree, however, lives on. The family is what is important and long-lasting. Your ancestors were the ones who built your world and gave you your personality and identity. Your children will carry that on and take care of you when you are old and bury you when you die. If God blesses you, many shoots will come from you that will grow into enormous limbs that will bear fruit and mature and grow. This is why we find prophecies that speak of the Messiah as the "branch."

> Behold, the days are coming, declares the LORD, when I will raise up for David a righteous Branch, and he shall reign as king and deal wisely, and shall execute justice and righteousness in the land. (Jer. 23:5)

> There shall come forth a shoot from the stump of Jesse,
> and a branch from his roots shall bear fruit. (Isa. 11:1)

The imagery here is that the family is a tree and the Messiah would be a "branch," a descendant of David's line. David's father was Jesse, so the Messiah could also be called a "shoot" from Jesse's line. Part of the imagery of the "shoot" is that when trees are cut back, they send out long, straight shoots from the base. These are used to make kings' scepters and tribal leaders' staffs.

This family-centric logic is behind the importance of all the "begats" of the Bible. In Genesis we meet the patriarchs of Israel and read the story of their growing clans. Explaining what each family was like and the relationships between families was critical to understanding society as a whole. That's why we find so many stories about the founders of each family in Genesis: they were key to each family's self-definition.

Where's the Romance Section?

If you walk into any bookstore, you'll find an enormous section called "romance," full of steamy love affairs. Even if you shop in the "mystery" or "adventure" sections, nearly every story will have a "love interest" as a subplot. It seems like no story can be told without it. How will the lonely hero find a soul mate and live happily ever after?

Our culture prioritizes finding romantic love, assuming that "living happily ever after" is the key to life well-lived.

Until you discover your one true love, you're filled with anxiety and self-questioning. So our culture resonates emotionally with this "redemption story of loneliness."

It might surprise you that we don't find much of this at all in the Bible. Not that we don't see passion, like in Song of Solomon. But for much of history marriages were arranged. Families decided who their children would marry. You had about as much choice in who would be your spouse as you did your brothers and sisters, but you grew to love them anyhow. The key to success in life wasn't to find a lover but to raise a bountiful family, a source of pride, love, and support when you got old.

Because of this, the Bible has a very different recurring emotional subplot—the "redemption story of barrenness." We see it over and over: Abraham and Sarah. Isaac and Rebekah. Jacob and Rachel. Hannah and Elkanah. Elizabeth and Zechariah. Each of them faces the awful fate of dying childless.

We point out how unfair it is that ancient society would see infertility as a sign of failure, but the rules of romance have harsh standards too. To compete at love, one must be attractive and charming. To be ugly or awkward is to be a social failure. Just ask anyone who's felt the rejection of being unable to get a date. Women felt their culture's shame more strongly then, and they feel shame more strongly in our culture too. But both sexes have never been immune to feeling like they don't measure up.

Once you have this in mind, the epic story of Abraham makes much more sense. He believed in God, but he and his wife Sarah were childless. God promised him the greatest of all blessings—a family that outnumbered the stars in the sky. But Abraham said, "What will you give me, for I continue childless?" in Genesis 15:2. The implications for Abraham are tragic. His whole life has been a waste because he has no family legacy. It doesn't matter if he owns vast numbers of servants and flocks—he will have died an utter failure.

This was the story that resonated with humanity down through the ages. Because of Abraham's unwavering faith, God promised him the greatest of blessings—that he would be the father of many nations. Can you imagine the nail-biting tension of those twenty-five years that he and Sarah waited for a son? And then the utter shock when God asked him to give Isaac back as an offering?

Because it was assumed that descendants would be like their forefathers, it made sense that Abraham would instill in his children his strong faith in God, and a great nation of believers would result. That's really the overall "plot" of the Bible—How would God fulfill his promise to Abraham, and how would this nation bless the whole world? That's where Jesus' "begats" really began.

The "sign" of the covenant, the physical remembrance, was circumcision, which has been required of all males from Abraham's time until this day. The choice of the sign wasn't coincidental. Rather, it marked the fact that the covenant was with Abraham's "seed," passed down through each generation of the family. Each time descendants are listed in the Bible, it shows that God has been honoring his side of the covenant.

Eunuchs for the Kingdom

One question has particularly puzzled Christians in recent years. Why doesn't the Bible ever discuss the idea of same-sex marriage, in either the Old or New Testament? We ask this question with our own cultural assumptions in the background. First, we assume that the overall goal of marriage is to satisfy romantic longings, and the purpose of a marriage covenant is to legitimize a sexual relationship. But throughout history, the purpose of marriage has been to covenantally establish a family, which would take care of its members when they got old and continue a family legacy. In a world where sterility was a disaster, marrying someone of the same sex was unthinkable.[2]

If having a family was so critical, why did both Jesus and Paul embrace the single life? Jesus certainly was strong on the permanence of marriage, forbidding divorce for any reason but adultery (Matt. 19:3–9). His disciples could see the difficulty of this command, and they wondered if it actually might be a better thing to not marry at all, a truly shocking idea in that culture. Jesus concurred, while noting that few will be able to accept a calling to singleness:

> Not everyone can receive this saying, but only those to whom it is given. For there are eunuchs who have been so from birth, and there are eunuchs who have been made eunuchs by men, and there are eunuchs who have made themselves eunuchs for the sake of the kingdom of heaven. Let the one who is able to receive this receive it. (vv. 11–12)

Here, Jesus used the term *eunuch* to refer to those who are denied the very things that brought meaning and success in life—family and children. He pointed out that some have that choice made for them by nature or by other people, but some made the choice themselves in order to devote themselves to serve God.

In using the word *eunuch*, Jesus likely had kingdom imagery in mind, because many kings appointed only eunuchs to high offices. In order to serve a king, these men had to give up the hope of having a family. The very word *eunuch* carried both of these implications. Besides referring to a castrated man, by the first century it also carried the connotation of being a high royal official (see Esth. 2:3; Dan. 1:3; Acts 8:27). Jesus was saying that in the same way, some will be called to forgo marriage to serve in God's kingdom. As shocking as this thought is in our culture, it would have been mind-boggling in Jesus' family-centric world.[3]

How could Jesus use *eunuch* in a positive way, considering that Deuteronomy 23:1 forbade eunuchs from entering the temple? Likely, Jesus was thinking in terms of a surprising promise that the prophet Isaiah had made about God's glorious eschatological kingdom:

> Let not the foreigner who has joined himself to the
>   Lord say,
>   "The Lord will surely separate me from his
>   people";
> and let not the eunuch say,
>   "Behold, I am a dry tree."
> For thus says the Lord:
> "To the eunuchs who keep my Sabbaths,
>   who choose the things that please me
>   and hold fast my covenant,
> I will give in my house and within my walls
>   a monument and a name
>   better than sons and daughters;
> I will give them an everlasting name
>   that shall not be cut off." (Isa. 56:3–5)

In a culture where the growth of one's family tree was the source of meaning in life, to be a eunuch was to be a withered, fruitless branch that might have leaves now but would soon be a lifeless stick. God, however, made an extravagant promise: he would welcome foreigners who had at one time worshiped other gods and even eunuchs who had served in their temples.

God's breathtaking declaration was that he would give eunuchs a "name better than sons and daughters" (v. 5). The word translated as "name" here really refers to "renown." (More about that in the next chapter.) One's success in life, one's "renown," was measured in terms of the legacy that a person left in his or her children. But in God's glorious kingdom, those who choose to serve him will receive an eternal legacy even more enduring than sons and daughters. He will graft them into his own family tree, and they will never be cut off.

Many of you who are reading this chapter struggle with broken families or crushed dreams of future family and are feeling left out of the whole "family" plot of the Bible. I write this chapter as a woman who is nearing fifty and has never married or had children. Personally, I will be among the first to ask the Lord to fulfill his promise to give the eunuchs who served him a "name better than sons and daughters."

Who's a Son of Abraham?

In the time of Jesus and Paul, there was quite a debate over who was a "son of Abraham," with the understanding that a person's salvation was linked to being a part of the covenantal family. John the Baptist warned people not to trust in their lineage when he said,

> Do not suppose that you can say to yourselves, "We have Abraham for our father"; for I say to you that from these stones God is able to raise up children to Abraham. (Matt. 3:9 NASB)

In John's Gospel, Jesus had a heated discussion with some leaders on this same topic.

> [Jesus said,] "I know that you are offspring of Abraham; yet you seek to kill me because my word finds no place in you. I speak of what I have seen with my Father, and you do what you have heard from your father."
>
> They answered him, "Abraham is our father." Jesus said to them, "If you were Abraham's children, you would be doing the works Abraham did, but now you seek to kill me, a man who has told you the truth that I heard from God. This is not what Abraham did. You are doing the works your father did." (John 8:37–41)

Behind this conversation is the idea that they were claiming to be part of the "saved" because Abraham was their father. Jesus questions this assumption, pointing out that if they were sons of Abraham, he would expect them to be like him. Instead, he says they are like their "father" Satan, the "father of lies."

In Paul's writing, too, he deals with the idea that being a "son of Abraham," a circumcised Jew, was necessary for salvation. Christians have traditionally read Paul's arguments over circumcision as a contrast between grace and legalism. But recent scholarship suggests that a greater issue was whether God would extend his salvation to those outside the family of Abraham.[4]

Jews of the first century were a small minority in the Roman Empire, and many had endured great persecution for not adopting Hellenistic ways. About 150 years before Christ, Jews were executed if they circumcised their sons in order to be faithful to God. As a reaction to the encroaching Gentile world, they put great emphasis on observing laws that separated them from Gentiles as a way to show their commitment to God.

Being circumcised was especially important because it marked them as "sons of Abraham" and part of the family covenant. To them, it undermined God's covenant with Abraham to extend it to others who had not become full proselytes to Judaism.

Surprisingly, Paul does not say that a person doesn't need to be a son of Abraham to be saved. Rather, he deals with this issue by redefining what a "son of Abraham" is, stretching the definition to include the Gentiles, the very group not included in the definition of a "son of Abraham"! He points out that Abraham himself was a Gentile, and that God's promise was given to him because of his faith, before he was circumcised.

> Is this blessedness only for the circumcised, or also for the uncircumcised? We have been saying that Abraham's faith was credited to him as righteousness. Under what circumstances was it credited? Was it after he was circumcised, or before? It was not after, but before! And he received circumcision as a sign, a seal of the righteousness that he had by faith while he was still uncircumcised. So then, he is the father of all who believe but have not been circumcised, in order that righteousness might be credited to them. (Rom. 4:9–11 NIV)

Abraham is the "father of all who believe but have not been circumcised," in the sense of being the archetype and prime example. He has "fathered" the very people that he did not father! In Galatians, Paul made a similar point:

> Even so Abraham believed God, and it was reckoned to him as righteousness. Therefore, be sure that it is those who are of faith who are sons of Abraham. The Scripture, foreseeing that God would justify the Gentiles by faith, preached the gospel beforehand to Abraham, saying, "All the nations (Gentiles, *goyim*) will be blessed in you." (Gal. 3:6–8)

Paul was interpreting the words of God's promise to Abraham to say that he would bless the *goyim* through him. He was pointing out that God's blessings were not just for his biological descendants who were circumcised but also for the Gentiles of the world. Yet they still come through Abraham's family.

From this, Paul inferred that Gentile believers in Jesus Christ were true "sons of Abraham." In his words from Galatians 3:28–29, he concluded:

> There is neither Jew nor Greek, slave nor free, male nor female, for you are all one in Christ Jesus. If you belong to Christ, then you are Abraham's descendants, and heirs according to the promise.

TOOLS AND REFLECTIONS

Reading

1. Read the parable of the prodigal son in Luke 15:11–32. In that culture of tightly knit, loyal families, what do

you think it said about a son if he demanded a large portion of his family's estate and then moved away? What do you think it said about the father in how he responded? Parents, if one of your children had done this, how would you respond?

2. Imagine writing a résumé of your achievements that is not based on your work life but rather on the expansion of your family. How successful have you been? How has this aspect of your life served God?

3. The firstborn son of a family was understood to be the "first fruits of [a man's] vigor" (Ps. 105:36 NASB), a sign of the father's virility and his ability to leave a powerful legacy. What does it say that God did not allow his blessing to be passed down to the firstborn sons of Abraham, Isaac, Jacob, Judah, Joseph, and David? How does this relate to Jesus?

4. Read Genesis 29:1–30:22 and Genesis 48–49 about the establishment of the family of Jacob. On a piece of paper, list the children born of each mother and her maidservant. These are the forefathers of the tribes of Israel. Who's most prominent? Which tribe is Jesus from? What was important about Jacob adopting Joseph's sons, Ephraim and Manassah?

Thoughts for Going Deeper

- In future Bible reading, watch what happens to Jacob's sons once they become tribes, and note where they end up on a map. Keep track of who was of Leah's family and who was of Rachel's family. These relationships will be key throughout Israel's history.

- A great movie to watch is *Fiddler on the Roof* (MGM, 1971), a classic musical about a Jewish family in Russia who experiences the encroachment of Western modernity on their family-centered traditions. Each daughter ignores her father's wishes and follows the whims of romance to choose a husband who distances her from her family more and more. Try watching the movie from a cultural perspective that emphasizes family loyalty over individual fulfillment. How does this add to the story?

7

✳ ✳ ✳

Reading the Bible as a "We"

Insights from a Communal Perspective

Did you know that you can now order a copy of a Bible translation called "*Your* Personalized Bible" which will insert your name in more than seven thousand verses?[1] Here are a few verses from my copy:

> Lois like a sheep has gone astray. Lois has turned to her own way; and the Lord has laid on Him Lois's iniquity. (Isa. 53:6)
>
> Lois is the light of the world. (Matt. 5:14)
>
> You have made Lois a little lower than God,
> And crowned Lois with glory and honor.
> You make Lois a ruler over the works of Your hands.
> You have put all things under Lois' feet. (Ps. 8:5–6)

You might think I'd be a fan of this style of study. I'm single, never married. I'm self-employed. I work by myself out of my own home office. I have no boss, no husband, no children. I'm queen of my own pleasant little world. I've heard the siren call of individualism and succumbed as much as anyone, so you'd think I'd want to read my Bible that way.

The more I study the Bible, however, the more I'm realizing the many ways that an individualistic approach misunderstands the text. Take, for instance, this Bible's translation of 1 Corinthians 3:16, "Lois is a temple of God." Often people read this line as saying, "Your body is a sacred 'deity-shrine' and you must pamper it accordingly." But Paul was not trying to convince us to apply more UV-blocking moisturizer or eat more vegetables. Rather, he was telling the Corinthians that *all together* they were the temple of God, and that they were being built together into one dwelling place for his Spirit. Pagans had many temples, but the true God had only one. They were the "house," the *bayit* that God had promised David—not just a structure but a lineage, a family. Paul's focus was not on each person individually but rather on the body of believers as a whole.[2]

This is only one of many errors we make. Consider the line, "Lois is the light of the world" (Matt. 5:14). Is this specifically about me, all by myself, or could Jesus have been addressing the whole faithful community? His very next words were, "A city on a hill cannot be hidden," picturing a village full of people, not just one person alone. Most of the time Jesus and Paul were speaking to groups and addressing them as a whole, not as individuals.

Part of the reason we read the biblical text as if it were addressed to "me personally" is because English only has one word, *you*, which can be either singular or plural. Unlike Greek, Hebrew, and many other languages, we can't distinguish whether a speaker is addressing one person or a group. As a result, English speakers have a habit of reading every "you" in the Bible as if it's addressed to "me all by myself" rather than "me within God's larger community."

American Southerners have an advantage here, because they use "y'all" when they address a group. Maybe the antidote to the "*Your* Personalized Bible" is to publish a "Southern-style" Bible where Jesus says, "Y'all are the light of the world," and Paul says, "Y'all are the temple of God," so that we'd know both were speaking to groups rather than to individuals.

Putting Away My Selfie Stick

Many modern readers like to picture themselves as if God is speaking to them alone when they read the Bible, to better feel the emotional impact of passages of conviction and encouragement. A few years ago, I used to do this too—mentally razor promises out of my Bible and see them as applicable only to myself. Any day I needed to, I'd find a personal pick-me-up, ignoring the people to whom they were actually given. (Hmm, funny—I didn't think to do this with the curses.) My version of "being there" was not unlike how many of us travel now, taking selfies everywhere we go. I was just using the biblical world as my backdrop instead.

I discovered a vastly more meaningful way to read God's promises a few years ago, on a rainy, blustery February day when I visited Yad VaShem, the Holocaust museum in Jerusalem. Mostly underground, the museum is shaped like an enormous spike bored through the mountaintop. Two massive concrete walls form a long, deep, triangular tunnel. Daylight enters only through a narrow skylight along the peak. As you wind your way through, the walls descend and narrow, as if you're in a constricting vice grip. It's impossible to avoid a sense of impending doom as the account unfolds of the horror the Jews experienced in Nazi Germany. Finally, as the tour concludes, the tunnel re-expands and ascends. A wall of tall glass doors opens onto a veranda overlooking the city, giving visitors a sense of hope at the end of the story.

Touring this memorial is a powerful experience any time, but that day the dismal weather amplified the experience. The raindrops felt like mourners' tears as our bus rolled up to the museum, and the gloomy, overcast sky added to the memorial's tomblike atmosphere. At the end of the tour, though, just as I emerged through the glass exit doors, the clouds parted and sunbeams burst through on a truly glorious scene. The forested, verdant hills of western Jerusalem dripped in the sunshine, refreshed and revitalized by the rainfall. I was overwhelmed as I realized that to a Jew who had endured the Holocaust, this scene would have been absolutely breathtaking, a stunning fulfillment of an impossible dream. Here before me lay the promised land that the Jewish people have longed for throughout their history.

This scene gave me a new perspective on Jeremiah 29:11, "'For I know the plans I have for you,' declares the Lord, 'plans to prosper you and not to harm you, plans to give you hope and a future'" (NIV), which I usually envision embroidered with a Precious Moments figure on a frilly pillow. Imagine hearing it in its original context, as it sounded to the Israelites who heard the words from Jeremiah's lips during the

Babylonian exile. The people had been torn from this beautiful land, and death and horror had consumed their nation. All God's promises seemed utterly undone. After seeing their world collapse, Jeremiah's words about God's plan to give his people "hope and a future" must have been absolutely breathtaking.

When I allowed God to make this promise to the ancient people of Israel instead of to me, I got to see God's tremendous, redemptive love. I discovered a God who is able to move mountains on behalf of his people. God's love was revealed on a far grander scale when I appreciated it in its context, rather than plucking out lines as my own, divorcing them from their original listeners.

To do that, though, I had to care about the concerns of a nation that I'd never met. This doesn't mean that God can't still speak to me in a personal way through a Bible verse. Goodness knows he often does. But I keep one eye on the original listeners all the while, trying to think about them too. As I praise God for his faithfulness to his people, it just convinces me all the more that he'll be faithful to me too.

Jesus advised his disciples to take the bottom spot when they arrived at a banquet until they were invited to move up (Luke 14:8–11). This seems to be applicable here. By mentally moving myself out of the center and letting Israel be the focus of the story, I can practice being Christlike in caring about the concerns of others over my own.

Thinking as a "We"

If you're like me, it is very hard to resonate with group-thinking. In the WEIRD study (see page 36), Americans were off the charts with respect to individualism. Our nation was formed from people who left family behind and braved an enormous ocean to live in an unknown land. It takes a lot of independence and optimistic self-reliance to be able to face life alone.

What we hear as children is "think for yourself" or "stand on your own two feet." Each one of us is responsible for his or her own success or failure. Indeed, we aren't seen as mature until we've "left the nest" and "cut the apron strings."

In contrast, much of the world emphasizes just the opposite, knowing the advantages of functioning as a tightly knit team. From his travels in Africa, Rysjard Kapuscinski writes:

> Individualism is highly prized in Europe, and perhaps nowhere more so than in America; in Africa, it is synonymous with unhappiness, with being accursed. African tradition is collectivism for only in a harmonious group could one face the obstacles thrown up by nature.[3]

You may recoil at living within a collectivist culture, cringing at the thought of the worst abuses: totalitarian regimes, brainwashed cults, or mindless mobs. But groups can be very positive too. Elite drum corps. Winning football teams. Well-run businesses. Loving families! On a good team, everyone contributes and is valued and accountable. Bad teams exploit weak members or use their power toward evil ends.

What children hear in collective cultures is, "Welcome to the family! You belong! You're a member of a family, a tribe, and a people. Together we will prosper! We are your team, your identity." The goal of life is to see your team succeed.

Your family and people mean everything to you, and your fate and theirs are intertwined. Their enemies are your enemies and their problems are your problems. Your priority is the success of your people rather than your own.

If, God forbid, you commit a crime, it wouldn't be just a personal failure, it would humiliate both you and your family, because you've let your whole community down. Obviously, your parents didn't teach you right from wrong! Group-oriented societies are much more concerned about public honor and shame than Western individualists, who think much more in terms of private guilt and personal sin.

What Does Your Name Mean?

International communications trainer Sarah Lanier has traveled the globe to teach about cultural differences. In her book *Foreign to Familiar*, she tells about how she handled some Arab boys who were taunting her with catcalls on the street one day. To their surprise, she turned and confronted them in Arabic, asking their family names. Answering sheepishly, the boys asked her why she wanted to know. Because, she replied, she would tell their fathers about their behavior and how they were being an embarrassment to their families. Horrified, the boys apologized profusely and pleaded with her not to do such a thing.[4]

Sarah Lanier asked the boys their names because she knew that their family's reputation, their "name," was of critical importance in their society. Knowing this helps us decode a much misunderstood word in our Bibles, the Hebrew word *shem*, which overlaps with the English word *name* but is actually much broader. We find "name" used in odd-sounding ways, like, "I will make you a name and a praise among all people of the earth" (Zeph. 3:20 KJV).

The key to the puzzle of *shem* is to consider the Bible's collective context. There, a person's identity within the wider community was of utmost significance. There, the word *shem* is much more about one's *identity within a community* than the verbal label that a person bears, like "George," "Bill," or "Mary," even though the word *shem* does mean "name" in that sense too.

Imagine that a stranger walks up to you and asks, "What's your identity?" You could answer by saying "Mary Smith," but your identity, your *shem*, is much bigger than that. It comes from your family, your education, your job, and how others perceive your status, your reputation, or your authority. To speak "in the name" of someone is to speak by his or her authority.

Notice that the name the Arab boys were worried about protecting was their *family name*, rather than their personal name. Here's a little thought experiment: What does your *last name*, your family name, say about you? (Think about your family reputation, not word origins or nationality.) If you grew up in a small town where everyone knows everyone, and families have been around for generations, it likely tells people a lot about you. Like it or not, your "name" connects you to the people who define you. It reminds people of everything your family has done in the past and forecasts what kind of person you will grow up to be.

For better or for worse, this little label can have great power. It can be wonderful if you are a Rockefeller or a Kennedy, or terrible if you are a Hitler or a Madoff. This one word can bestow enormous influence upon you or brand you as a reviled outcast, irrespective of anything you've ever done in life.[5]

If this is true in our society, just imagine how much more true it would be in a culture where community is everything, where people can't just leave town to start over with a clean slate. How you are viewed by wider society is absolutely critical to your identity as a person. Your name precedes you . . . everywhere.

Collectivist cultures that emphasize "honor" and "shame" are really thinking in terms of *shem* in the biblical sense. To have a "great name" is to be well-known and influential, and to have a "bad name" is to be an embarrassment to everyone who knows you. This is why the word *shem* is sometimes translated as *fame*, *renown*, *reputation*, *authority*, or *honor* rather than *name*.[6] See how it clarifies these verses:

Zephaniah 3:20	
I will make you a name and a praise among all people of the earth. (KJV)	*I will make you renowned* and praised among all the peoples of the earth. (ESV)
Joshua 9:9	
From a very distant country your servants have come, *because of the name* of the LORD your God. (ESV)	Your servants have come from a very distant country *because of the fame* of the LORD your God. (NIV)
Nehemiah 6:13	
So they could *give me a bad name* in order to taunt me. (ESV)	So *provide them a scandal* with which to reproach me. (NJPS)
Isaiah 55:13	
Instead of the thorn shall come up the fir tree . . . and *it shall be to the LORD for a name*, for an everlasting sign that shall not be cut off. (KJV)	Instead of the thornbush will grow the juniper. . . . *This will be for the LORD's renown*, for an everlasting sign, that will endure forever. (NIV)

In collective, hierarchical cultures, one's "name" is closely associated with honor and authority. When the Scriptures talk about God giving a person a "new name," it denotes that they are being *given a new status* in society. Abram, a withered-up wanderer, became *Abraham*, father of nations! Sarai, a barren old matron, became *Sarah*, mother of princes! God changed their identity and gave them a new role in society, and it came with a change in name.

In a communal society, rejecting your family heritage will cost you dearly and even cause you to be expelled from your community. Years ago, I was enjoying a lovely dinner with Christian friends who lived in Jerusalem. Another guest they had invited was active in their congregation, and he looked obviously Jewish. To start a conversation, I tossed out a question: "So . . . what did your family say when you told them you had become a Christian?"

Foolish me. It was like a bomb had dropped in the room.

After an awkward silence, our hostess delicately changed the subject. Later, she explained that when their friend told his parents about his faith in Christ, his father "sat shiva," meaning that he observed the seven days of mourning at a person's death. This has been the response of Jews down through the centuries because of the enormous persecution they've undergone at the hands of Christians. Because of his faith, this young man had been disowned by his family.

In many cultures, accepting Christ means giving up one's family, heritage, prestige, and any chance of success. This is why Christ promises to give a "new name" to his followers who refuse to deny him in the face of persecution (Rev. 2:17). In this world they may have forfeited their "name," their reputation, for his sake. But when he comes to reign in glory, these are the people whom he will single out for acclaim. No more will they be known as outcasts but as leaders and princes, with renown to replace the shame they bore during their lives.

God's Communal Commands

Modern readers find many of the Old Testament laws confusing, because we assume their moral basis is on an individual level and we overlook their communal implications. For instance, one perplexing law is to not make garments of both wool and linen (Deut. 22:11). Why was it given?

According to Jewish scholar Jacob Milgrom, it was because of how it differentiated the priestly part of the community.[7] Because both the priestly garments and the tabernacle weavings were a combination of wool and linen, it was prohibited for laypersons to dress in the same way. Another prohibited mixture had the same rationale. No one but the priests could blend together aromatic spices in the same combination that was used to make sacred anointing oil (Exod. 30:33). The Israelites were fresh from a polytheistic world and strongly tempted to set up private, do-it-yourself shrines to offer a few sacrifices on the side, so they were barred from dressing like priests or duplicating certain items used in worship.

We actually have similar laws today. Did you realize that it's illegal to dress up in a badge and a uniform to impersonate a police officer? The police are authorized to stop a car, break down a door, or handcuff a person—things no one else may do. Likewise, God had given priests the authority to lead worship, and they had to be noticeably different from everyone else.

Israel's feasts were inherently communal events. Through them, God was instructing the Israelites to gather together and rejoice in his presence, celebrating their corporate relationship with God. You might be surprised by the communal implications of the Sabbath law too. Christians assume that it is addressed to each person individually. But listen to Exodus 23:12:

> Six days you shall do your work, but on the seventh day you shall rest; that your ox and your donkey may have rest, and the son of your servant woman, and the alien, may be refreshed.

Take note of the emphasis here. Who is supposed to be refreshed when the people of Israel observe the Sabbath? It's the *animals* and the *servants* and the *aliens*.

Doesn't that seem illogical? That doesn't make sense if this command is addressed to each person individually. In order to understand it, you need to think *communally*. Landowners were being addressed, and whole households were the focus of the command. *As a community you shall rest*, so that your servants and even your animals can be refreshed too.

In that society, there was no way that animals and servants could observe the Sabbath without the permission of their owners. If a farmer decided that it was a good day for plowing, his servants and animals had little choice but to obey him. Aliens or "sojourners" were just as powerless, working as migrant laborers and hired help for others.

According to this verse, the refreshment of Sabbath was primarily intended for the *ones who could not rest* without the permission of others. Elsewhere, the Sabbath was linked to remembering how the Israelites had once been slaves in Egypt who never got to rest:

> You shall not do any work, you or your son or your daughter or your male servant or your female servant, or your ox or

> your donkey or any of your livestock, or the sojourner who is within your gates, that your male servant and your female servant may rest as well as you. You shall remember that you were a slave in the land of Egypt, and the LORD your God brought you out from there with a mighty hand and an outstretched arm. Therefore the LORD your God commanded you to keep the Sabbath day. (Deut. 5:14–15)

This connection is obscured when the word *eved* is translated two different ways into English, as "male servant" in verse 14 but as "slave" in verse 15. In Hebrew, you must release your *eved* because you were once an *eved*. The reason that Israel must release others from work is to remember how God had done the same for them!

Understood in this way, the Sabbath parallels other commands of ceasing and release that come in sevens. Every seven years Israel was to forgive debts and release slaves. Every forty-nine years they were supposed to return the land to those who had sold it during times of hardship.

When you realize how foundational the Sabbath was to Israel's radical social ethics, it's really quite stunning. All of life's rhythms were to revolve around celebrating the indescribable joy of the day when the whips ceased cracking, the shackles fell off, and the cell doors swung open toward freedom. Week after week, season after season, year after year, God was commanding Israel to remember his extravagant, rescuing love by extending that redemption to others.

During Jesus' ministry, he also stressed that the appropriate response to God's forgiveness is to extend it to others. If we've been forgiven a debt of ten thousand talents, we can't shake down our debtors for a few denarii. We are to forgive as we have been forgiven, just as Israel was to release others in order to remember its own release from bondage. When we realize our sin and how much we have been set free from, and we share this overwhelming forgiveness with others, God will fill our lives with his love.

Abraham, Incorporated

Many of us read our Bibles as a collection of stories of individuals and their personal encounters with God. We swim through a sea of dull details, aiming for islands of solitary, one-on-one conversations with God because they are all we relate to.

Adam and Eve and God
Abraham and God
Moses and God
David and God

A reader from a communal culture, however, would notice that Scripture frames itself collectively, in terms of the family of Abraham and the kingdom of Christ.

As hard as Westerners find it to relate to collective cultures, we actually do think more communally in the business world. Consider what happens when you're hired into a company. You're handed a box of business cards emblazoned with your name and the corporate logo, and sometimes a company shirt too. Suddenly you're expected to become the face of the company to the world. If you do a bad job, the company's reputation will suffer and yours will too. Ultimately, your fate is tied to the company—if it prospers, so do you, and if it fails, you'll also fail.

Maybe we could relate better to our Bibles if we put on our "corporate world" hats and looked at the biblical story as that of "Abraham, Inc.," a business partnership between God and Abraham, founded to publicize its divine corporate owner and his grand vision of "Holiness and Justice for All."

God promised Abraham that one day this family business would transform the world! It's hard, though, to imagine how a mom-and-pop venture like this would even survive in a dog-eat-dog business climate with massive conglomerates like Egypt Megacorp, Babylon Multinational, and, later, Rome Unlimited. Hostile Philistine competitors with Advanced Iron Technology also threaten takeover.

As you follow the story, you see how more problems come from within the company. Management is, at times, corrupt. Employees want to replace God's "Holiness and Justice for All" vision with a more saleable product, "Fertile Fields and Phallic Fun," which has been popular for their competitor, Baal, Inc. At one point God even insists on a corporate purge.

Finally, God, the deity-owner, promises to send in his own son to take charge as CEO and bring the company back in line with his plans. The board of directors, however, opposes his plan and plots to have his son bumped off instead. How will this scrappy little start-up achieve God's outsized vision? Find out yourself in this spine-tingling corporate thriller.

Hoping for a Game-Saving Quarterback

Because of our individualism we also overlook a major issue on the minds of everyone in the Gospels: Israel, God's covenant family. Notice that *Israel*, as I'm using the word here, does not refer to the modern country, or to politics, or to any kind of detached, historical reference to a nation. Here I'm speaking in terms of the "family of Abraham" as the main character of the biblical story.

We hear this theme over and over surrounding Jesus' birth and dedication at the temple. John's father, Zechariah, begins his praises with, "Blessed be the Lord God of Israel, for he has visited and redeemed his people" (Luke 1:68). Simeon, too, rejoices over the newborn Jesus that God has sent "a light for revelation to the Gentiles, and for glory to your people Israel" (2:32). Everyone is focused on what God has done for his covenant family, the people of Israel.

Fast-forward to Jesus' conversation on the Emmaus road, and the issue that consumed Cleopas and his companion was their forlorn hope that "he was the one to redeem Israel" (24:21). What he was hoping was that God had finally sent in a winning quarterback who would make the game-saving play for Team Israel. The punch line that Jesus gave him is "Yes, he has!" But it happened in a way that Cleopas didn't quite understand. More about this later.

If you want to "be there" alongside Jesus' Jewish disciples, in some sense you need to care about Israel as *your* family, whom you hold precious and dear. Just imagine, by some amazing grace, your relatives were the ones whom the true God covenanted with to proclaim himself to the world. When your family prospered, it showed God's power, and when they were oppressed, God looked like a loser too. God's fate is tied up with your fate. It's galling and shocking to you how the world sees the God of Israel as a wimpy, pathetic deity when he's the true Creator of the world. When is he going to be rightly acknowledged as the world's true King?

Every day it pains you to see your family languishing, oppressed by rock-worshiping idolaters. Not just for your own sake, but because God's reputation is being dragged through the mud.

Too easily we condemn Jesus' contemporaries for longing for a Messiah who is a military leader, a true Son of David. Put yourself in their shoes, though. They've been longing and praying for God's reign to be established over the world, and how else is he going to do it but by winning the war with their enemies? After all, that was how he originally redeemed the nation from Egypt, when he slew Pharaoh's oncoming army. The whole ancient world trembled when they heard the report. The prophets had made promise after promise that God would do the same again. When, oh when, would he fulfill his own words?

Jesus, of course, came to redeem his people in a very different way, and many in Israel rejected him, especially among their leaders. Some embraced him as God's Messiah nonetheless. Yet it was painful for Paul and other Jewish believers to think that God would save only some of his covenant family and not all of it. Paul grieved with great sorrow and unceasing anguish in his heart, and wished he could be accursed for the sake of his brothers (Rom. 9:2–3).

This was the burning issue for Paul in his letter to the Romans. Not only was it scandalous that not every Jew would embrace God's Messiah but it was beyond stunning to think that God would adopt Gentiles as his people, and even fill them with his Holy Spirit, without their embracing the family covenant he had given to the people of Israel on Mount Sinai. This turn of events was radical and shocking indeed.

When the Many Are One

I told you that because we can't see the plural "you" in English, we miss when the biblical text is speaking collectively. In fact, even if you can find the "y'alls," you'll still be missing some things, because many places when the Bible is using a singular "you," it is actually still speaking collectively, to a whole group. Not just to each person individually in the crowd but to all of them together. The famous command, "You shall love the LORD your God with all your heart" (Deut. 6:5), is actually a command to the *person* of Israel—that, as a nation, Israel must love God with all its heart.

Often, an ancestor's name was used interchangeably with the group. For instance, "You drink wine by the bowlful and use the finest lotions, but you do not grieve over the ruin of Joseph" (Amos 6:6 NIV). "Joseph" referred to the two tribes that came from Joseph, his sons Ephraim and Manassah, which were the northern tribes that were destroyed by Assyria.

The ancestor or leader of a people is often pictured as one with the group as a collective whole. In Genesis 28:14, the Lord promised Jacob, "Your offspring shall be like the dust of the earth, and you [singular] shall spread abroad to the west and to the east and to the north and to the south, and in you and your offspring shall all the families of the earth be blessed." It's as if Jacob himself will do the spreading out.

Jewish scholar Michael Fishbane points out that the imagery here is that *all together they are one person*.[8] This style of addressing a group as if they are one person is especially common in Deuteronomy and Isaiah. The New Testament similarly talks about us as being "one body" or "in Christ." This is part of Paul's logic when he preaches that "as by a man came death, by a man has come also the resurrection of the dead" (1 Cor. 15:21). Some have assumed that this communal identity was novel to the New Testament, not realizing that it permeates the Scriptures of Israel as well.

The Illogical Logic of Mercy

Do you remember *The Lion, the Witch and the Wardrobe* by C. S. Lewis? At the story's climax, the White Witch demands the life of the boy Edmund because he is a traitor to his family. She says that the "deep magic" allows her to kill every traitor—his life is forfeit for his sin. Aslan, the Lion who represents Christ, gives his life in the boy's place but later rises from the dead. When asked why, he said,

> There is a magic deeper still which [the White Witch] did not know . . . that when a willing victim who had committed no treachery was killed in a traitor's stead, the Table [of judgment] would crack and Death itself would start working backward.[9]

This "deeper magic" of Narnia—the idea that the sins of one person can be forgiven because of another person's sacrifice—is a fundamental part of the Christian understanding of substitutionary atonement. We take it for granted that mercy is shown to the guilty for the sake of an innocent person. If you think about it, though, this is quite illogical. In our own relationships we generally don't transfer our feelings from one person to another. We don't say "thank you" to one person because someone else did us a favor. But somehow we have gotten used to the idea that God will forgive many sinners because of the righteousness of just one person.

Does the idea of granting mercy for the sake of another have precedent in the Hebrew Scriptures? One might think it was invented in the New Testament. But interestingly, according to Jewish scholars, the answer is yes. Many have found this merciful "divine illogic" throughout the Old Testament and consider it an important principle of Judaism! When these scholars explore the minute details of the Torah and Hebrew Scriptures, they often notice subtle themes that Christians miss.

Nahum Sarna sees this pattern as early as Genesis 19, when Lot was saved from the destruction of Sodom. Lot had chosen to move to Sodom despite knowing that it was sinful. He became active in city leadership and even allowed his daughters to intermarry with the population. Even though Lot wasn't as corrupt as the Sodomites, God did not save him because of his own righteousness. Rather, the Bible says that "God was mindful of Abraham and removed Lot from the midst of the upheaval" (Gen. 19:29 NJPS). God delivered Lot from the catastrophe for the sake of Abraham—as a response to Abraham's faithfulness, not Lot's. According to Sarna,

> This "doctrine of merit" is not an infrequent theme in the Bible and constitutes many such incidents in which the righteousness of chosen individuals may sustain other individuals or even an entire group through its protective power.[10]

The Merit of the Fathers

A related idea is that of *zechut avot* (ze-KHUT ah-VOTE), the "merit of the fathers," that God would show special mercy toward the people of Israel because of the merits of their forefathers Abraham, Isaac, and Jacob.[11] They see this as coming from God's promises to the patriarchs, and because God told Moses that he would pardon to the thousandth generation those who love him (see Exod. 34:6–7). When Moses appealed to God to forgive the rebellious Israelites in the wilderness, he reminded God of his promise to his ancestors (Exod. 32:13; Deut. 9:27). In Micah 7, God's mercy is also linked to his pledge to the patriarchs:

> Who is a God like you,
> who pardons sin and forgives the transgression
> of the remnant of his inheritance?
> You do not stay angry forever
> but delight to show mercy.
> You will again have compassion on us;
> you will tread our sins underfoot
> and hurl all our iniquities into the depths of the sea.
> You will be faithful to Jacob,
> and show love to Abraham,
> as you pledged on oath to our ancestors
> in days long ago. (Mic. 7:18–20 NIV)

Even Paul alludes to this idea in Romans 11:28–29: "but as far as election is concerned, they are loved on account of the patriarchs, for God's gifts and his call are irrevocable" (NIV). John the Baptist, however, told his audience to repent and to not assume that the merit of their ancestors would be sufficient to pay for their sins: "Do not think you can say to yourselves, 'We have Abraham as our father.' I tell you that out of these stones God can raise up children for Abraham" (Matt. 3:9 NIV).

On Rosh Hashanah and Yom Kippur, when Jews pray for forgiveness for their sins, the focus is on the *Akedah*, the

"Binding of Isaac," the Genesis 22 account of Abraham's willingness to sacrifice Isaac at God's request. Remarkably, some traditional prayers ask for forgiveness for the sake of Abraham, who was a father who had such great love for God that he was willing to sacrifice his own son. Others even petition for mercy for the sake of Isaac, who offered himself up as a willing sacrifice! (They point out that if Isaac was carrying enough wood to burn a sacrifice, he had to be a grown man and easily able to overpower his elderly father. His willingness to be a sacrifice is seen as a prominent theme of the story.)[12]

While these prayers do not explicitly name Christ, they do show that the Jewish reading of the Hebrew Bible supports the idea that a sinner can seek forgiveness from God because of the righteous merits of another person.

Jesus' first followers were well acquainted with the Hebrew Scriptures and their interpretation. They certainly knew that Isaiah spoke of one who would "[bear] the sin of many, and [make] intercession for the transgressors" (Isa. 53:12 NIV). They did not invent the idea that Jesus' sacrifice would atone for the sins of those who believed in him. Rather, they saw that it was woven through their Scriptures from beginning to end. We'll look at this in a little more depth later.

The Gospel of the Kingdom

Another word that causes individualists difficulty is *kingdom*, even though Jesus preached absolutely nonstop about the kingdom. I used to think of "kingdom" as a very esoteric, abstract idea, not considering the fact that the word *kingdom* describes a *community*. It's describing God's relationship with a whole group of people whom he is redeeming. When we look for the "gospel" in the Gospels we search for an individual message of salvation. Instead, Jesus was speaking in terms of redeeming *a whole people*.

Consider—if "Christ" means "God's appointed King," it implies that he rules over a kingdom, a body of people. To "accept Christ" is to "enter his kingdom," an inherently plural action. The main focus of his earthly ministry was to announce what God was doing on earth to redeem an entire people for himself.

Back in the early 2000s, bestselling vampire-genre novelist Anne Rice made a splash by publicly announcing that she had become a Christian. A few years later, however, she announced that because she disagreed on various social issues, she was leaving the church. She pledged that she was still committed to her faith in God.

If you grasp the communal nature of salvation, you realize that this is inherently impossible. You can't quit the kingdom without quitting the King. You may be a solitary, do-nothing member who disagrees with everyone on every issue and never darkens a church's doorway, but you're still a part of the body of Christ, no matter what you do.

Paul preaches a creative anatomy lesson about the body to the Corinthians who were squabbling over spiritual gifts. Humorously, he re-imagines the body as one big eyeball that can't hear, or an enormous ear that can't smell. All people can't all have the same gifting, just as a body needs all sorts of different organs.

I wonder if Paul could preach another anatomical sermon if he saw us today. My sister Maureen has Type I diabetes, meaning that her pancreas has stopped making insulin. She's perpetually stabbing her fingertips and squeezing out drops of blood to check her sugar levels, and then jabbing herself with shots of insulin. She must monitor every mouthful she eats and can't ever take a day off from this tiresome routine. Wearily, Maureen tells me, "Lois, it's really hard to be your own pancreas." Because one of her organs has gone AWOL, it's thrown its burden on the rest of her body.

In America, our individualism makes us ever more prone to privatized faith. A growing number of people see participation in the church as unnecessary and decide to drop out. Lots of tissues and organs in its body have decided to quit, and the rest of the church body struggles to function without them. Why do we wonder when it does poorly?

What Can We-Thinking Teach Us?

As much as it seems like individualism defines us, I've discovered one form of group-thinking we still engage in quite regularly. I call it "they-thinking," where all the members of a group are seen as a whole and the group is assumed to think and act as one whole mass. It sounds almost absurd, but it's not uncommon when we get angry. Stereotypes and racism are products of this evil type of corporate thinking which focuses on pitting "us" against "them."

A tragic example is the libelous slur that has been leveled at Jews down through the ages by Christians: "Christ killer." It sounds almost nonsensical to individualists. Why would you accuse a Jewish person living today of a murder that occurred millennia ago? This slur only makes sense when you imagine an entire group acting as a seamless whole.

Christians are horrified when they discover how common anti-Semitism has been in our history, and then recognize that this attitude has robbed us of important insights about Jesus. What should we do?

Once again I see different types of responses. One is that of an individualist, who assumes, "It's not my problem because I didn't personally do it." The next is that of a "they-thinker," who gets very angry at how the church has sinned by cutting itself off from its Jewish roots. Some even accuse the church of the same kind of collective guilt that was used to accuse the Jewish people! Angrily they drop out—forgetting that, as followers of Christ, *they themselves* are a part of the group they are accusing.

The best response, I've found, is that of a "we-thinker" who says, "I too am connected with the people of my past, and I mourn over how we've persecuted the Jewish people." A "we-thinker" will ask, "How can I help my people change? How can I learn more? What can I do to share this rich heritage with my fellow Christians?"

TOOLS AND REFLECTIONS

Reflection: Introducing Yourself as Part of a "We"

Nowadays, we introduce ourselves individually, by talking about our work, education, or personal interests. Try considering how you might define yourself in terms of a collective identity instead. Use the questions below as creative suggestions for thinking collectively.

1. I am ________ (first name) of the clan of __________ (last name).

2. My tribe worships________ (give the name(s) of the god or gods you worship, whether they are Yahweh, Jesus, Baal, Allah, Mammon, etc.). You may just want to say "the true God of heaven and earth, the Lord God Almighty." (See Jon. 1:8–9 for how Jonah introduces himself.)

3. I am of the people of _______________ (geographical group that you see as your "people," whether it is Detroit, or Michigan, or America, etc.). Has your clan migrated from some other area to join this people?

4. My family are ___________ (list some defining characteristics of your family). Do you come from a family of merchants, farmers, musicians, builders, or preachers? Do you have an ancestor who was known for some great deed? (Married women, feel free to list the characteristics of your own family or your husband's family.)

5. I am the ______ (firstborn, second, third) son/daughter of _______________ (father's first name). My father was the (firstborn, second, third) son in the tribe of ___________ (last name). (Note: firstborn sons are very highly esteemed!) Married women: answer above with, "I am the wife of ____________, the (firstborn, second, third) son in the tribe of ____________ (last name)."

6. I am the father/mother of ______ (#) children and of ______ (#) grandchildren. (This, of course, is a source of great honor. If you are a grandmother or grandfather of a mighty clan, you deserve high acclaim indeed!) What differences do you feel when you define yourself as part of a group?

7. What teams have you been on in your life? What do you value in team members? How can this challenge how you live and serve on Christ's "kingdom team"?

8. Do you have a family name that gives you a reputation you did not earn yourself?

Thoughts for Going Deeper

- Check out the excellent chapters on individualism/collectivism as well as shame/honor in *Misreading Scripture with Western Eyes* by E. Randolph Richards and Brandon J. O'Brien (Downers Grove, IL: InterVarsity Press, 2012), 95–136, for more insights and an excellent discussion.
- Jackson Wu's discussion of how the gospel is communicated in China is remarkably perceptive to the Bible's collective context. See his book *One Gospel for all Nations: A Practical Approach to Biblical Contextualization* (Pasadena, CA: William Carey Library, 2015).

8

Like Grasshoppers in Our Own Eyes

Learning to "Think Small"

One night you have a dream. You are floating in the utter blackness of deep space. An eternity seems to pass, but nothing changes. It's just you and the velvety, dark, star-sprinkled sky.

Far off in the remote distance you notice a tiny disk of light. Squinting, you see it slowly unfurl into a spangled, spinning puddle of stars. Somehow you know this is the Milky Way. For eons you drift slowly toward the glowing, expanding mass.

Scanning its starry arms, you hope against hope that you can pick out an insignificant dot that you've known all your life as the "sun." For some reason, you seem to be attracted to a dim pinpoint buried in an arm about two thirds of the way out.

After drifting closer to the little dot for many millennia, you are finally so near you can see planets! You spot a tiny

Saturn with rings and then make out Jupiter with its red spot.

Your heart leaps to see a blue-green marble appear.

Slowly the spinning orb grows larger. Continents and oceans become visible under a blanket of clouds. As you descend through the stratosphere, mountain ranges and deserts flash past.

Now, below, you see splashes of light—cities aglow by night. Orienting yourself toward home, you feel yourself slowing as you fall. Through some amazing miracle, you gently land on your own front lawn!

Then you wake up, go outside, and look up at the night sky.

You realize that the scene you dreamed isn't make-believe. Unbelievably, this is reality. Every night that you look up into the starry, black sky, you're peering into the farthest reaches of the universe. You are but one single inhabitant out of billions in this world, and even the earth is a speck within the scope of the wider universe.

You are mind-bogglingly infinitesimal.

As obvious as this is, our smallness is not something people spend much time pondering nowadays. With each new Hubble telescope image and NASA mission in the news, you'd think we'd be more dumbfounded with awe.

You might be surprised to learn that the biblical world was much more aware of this reality than we are. According to Jewish biblical scholar James Kugel, the Hebrew Bible is permeated, like the rest of the ancient world, with a fundamental sense of humility and "smallness of self."[1] A common theme in ancient writings is that human beings are a small part of a larger system, at the mercy of forces much greater than themselves. Not only are they tiny in comparison to the vastness of the desert and ocean, they are helpless to prevent storms, droughts, plagues, and other natural disasters. They are also inconsequential in comparison with the whims of the gods and demons around them. Only by banding together can they hope to survive.

This sense of smallness is at the very core of Israel's consciousness of God, and it forms the very essence of biblical worship. The psalms and prophecies overflow with imagery of the tininess of humanity and God's utter magnificence in comparison:

> Do you not know?
> Have you not heard?
> Has it not been told you from the beginning?
> Have you not understood since the earth was founded?
> He sits enthroned above the circle of the earth,
> and its people are like grasshoppers. (Isa. 40:21–22 NIV)

> As a father shows compassion to his children,
> so the Lord shows compassion to those who fear him.
> For he knows our frame;
> he remembers that we are dust.
> As for man, his days are like grass;
> he flourishes like a flower of the field;
> for the wind passes over it, and it is gone,
> and its place knows it no more. (Ps. 103:13–16)

> "For my thoughts are not your thoughts,
> neither are your ways my ways,"
> declares the Lord.

> "As the heavens are higher than the earth,
> so are my ways higher than your ways
> and my thoughts than your thoughts." (Isa. 55:8–9 NIV)

It does seem remarkable, doesn't it? Technology has shown us in more detail than ever before the immensity of the universe and our microscopic existence within it, yet we have little sense of humility as a result.

We assume that as the centuries go by, our increasing knowledge is causing us to grow more intellectually sophisticated. But Kugel wonders whether modernity has actually dulled our senses to reality, one that biblical peoples had no problems experiencing. He writes that "something, a certain way of perceiving, has gradually closed inside of us, so that nowadays most people simply do not register, or do not have access to, what had been visible in an earlier age."[2] We are the ones who are numb and insensitive, unable to feel awe and wonder.

Our culture is so dazzled by its own brilliance that it's blinded to anything bigger than itself. We're like Cub Scouts on our first overnight camping trip. If we'd patiently wait out in the darkness, our eyes would gradually sensitize to nebulae and globular clusters and remote galaxies. Instead we're goofing around with our fancy new flashlights and giggling inside our pup tents. When we finally look up at the sky, we can't even make out the Milky Way.

Rabbi Abraham Heschel concurs, declaring that modern readers lack an ability to appreciate the grandeur of God.

> Greeks learned in order to comprehend. Hebrews learned in order to revere. The modern man learns in order to use. . . . To the modern man everything seems calculable; everything

> reducible to a figure. He has supreme faith in statistics and abhors the idea of a mystery. Obstinately he ignores the fact that we are all surrounded by things which we apprehend but cannot comprehend; that even reason is a mystery to itself. He is sure of his ability to explain all mystery away.
>
> The awareness of grandeur and the sublime is all but gone from the modern mind. . . . The sense for the sublime, the sign of the inward greatness of the human soul and something which is potentially given to all men, is now a rare gift. Yet without it, the world becomes flat and the soul a vacuum.[3]

Man Is Very Big and God Is Very Far Away

Our sense of our own "bigness" doesn't come so much from technology but rather from our Western perspective. Greek-thinking Westerners, particularly academics, read their Bible with an enormous sense of self, as if humans are capable of systematically predicting the thoughts and actions of a Being infinitely greater than ourselves.

We begin by assuming it's perfectly reasonable to boil down God's essence into a list of attributes, to effectively reduce him to a force, a vector defined by magnitude and direction. Then we weigh God's motives on our scales of justice and demand he make an accounting of himself. Of course, we are fully capable of grasping all of God's purposes and ends! Never mind the fact that Job had a conversation with God in which he learned just the opposite.

Western Christians spend a lot of time on theological speculation and find it surprising that Jewish thought does not. Rather, discussions focus much more on understanding how humanity is called to live according to God's will.[4]

Kugel comments that much of the Middle East, both Arabs and Jews, shares a cultural sense of "smallness" toward God. Little phrases in the language hint at the humility humankind should have in response to God's sovereignty. In Arabic, for instance, it's unthinkable to talk about one's distant future plans without adding the phrase "*inshallah*," "God willing." In Hebrew, Jews will add "*B'ezrat HaShem*," "with the help of God." Kugel shares the following story:

> Once I had the occasion to hear an Iraqi Jew describe the culture shock he experienced when, as a young man, he was forced to leave his native Baghdad to settle in the West. "In Baghdad," he said, "there were all kinds of people, some very traditional, some—like my own family—modern. . . . But all of us, modern and traditional, knew one thing: God is very big and man is very little. Once, some years after I had left Baghdad and moved to Western society, I went one evening to hear a famous theologian speak. I hoped that he would give me some piece of wisdom. But the more he spoke, the more his ideas and my own swirled around together in my head and the more upset I became. I could not get out of my mind this new thought: Man is very big, and God is very far away."[5]

The Wonderful Wizard

Remember *The Wizard of Oz*? When I was five, I ran and hid behind the couch every time I spotted the Wicked Witch, with her gnarled, bony fingers and screechy "I'll get you, my pretty!" The only thing more terrifying than her was the thundering, smoking presence of the "Great and Terrible Oz." Until, of course, Toto pulled aside the curtain to reveal that the Wizard was nothing more than a carnival huckster putting on a show.

This tale of theological disillusionment strikes a chord in many of us today. As we grow up and see the harshness of life, in a season of doubt we wonder if humankind might be all that exists and religious faith a mere projection. Maybe God is just smoke and mirrors, a product of our own delusion.

Kugel makes a surprising observation from his study of the ancient world: no one ever seriously entertained the idea that God didn't exist. He notes that the Bible doesn't hesitate to report people's doubts. Sometimes God's enemies mock him, and his followers complain that he does not punish evildoers or respond to those who suffer. But nowhere do we ever hear anyone wonder, "Well, maybe God just doesn't exist." No angry blasphemer ever bothers to consider the possibility that humanity just invented the idea of God—that we're all alone in the world. Kugel writes,

> Apparently, such a thought just never occurred to the blasphemers in question, nor to anyone else. On the contrary, God's being and fundamental nature seem everywhere simply to be assumed, a fact so well-known as to require no further elaboration. For the same reason, it would seem, the Bible does not begin by defining God or demonstrating His presence in reality. There must have been no need.[6]

Why not? Certainly it wasn't because they lived idyllic lives. They faced disease, warfare, famine, and other realities as stark and cruel as any today. Job was not alone in protesting against the tragedies that God allowed in the world. But nowhere do we find Job wondering if God simply didn't exist.

The Israelites were also not so primitive that they were incapable of skepticism, Kugel adds. The prophets jeered at the sheer idiocy of carving half of a wood block into an idol to worship when the other half would be chopped up as fuel for a cooking fire (Isa. 44:19).

Something else was going on entirely—a seismic shift in perception between their worldview and ours today. Throughout the Bible, the overall assumption is that humankind is only a tiny part of a much grander reality. Humans are weak, at the mercy of forces much greater than we are. We are *fundamentally* small.

When Westerners open Genesis, we struggle with the Bible's lack of proof that God exists. But in the biblical world, this simply wasn't a question on anyone's mind. From the perspective of the ancients, it was simply inconceivable that a puny human brain could be the ultimate source of God's existence.

Israel Is Small Potatoes Too

Another thing to keep in mind is that not only did biblical peoples see themselves as "small" but the people of Israel saw their entire nation as "little" too. Israel was perennially the ninety-eight-pound weakling getting sand kicked in its face by the bullying nations around it. Throughout its history, it was sandwiched between the superpowers of the ancient world like Egypt and Babylon, and continually invaded and oppressed by foreign armies like the Assyrians, Greeks, and Romans.

This small-potatoes thinking is especially obvious when the Israelites left Egypt and first arrived on the cusp of the promised land. When God invited them to survey Canaan's bounty, they found huge clusters of grapes that they hauled back on poles between two men. You'd think they'd be bursting with confidence at this amazing gift they were being given. Instead, they were terrified. The land might be rich and its fruit enormous, but the residents were giants! The Israelites wailed, "We seemed to ourselves like grasshoppers, and so we seemed to them" (Num. 13:33). Instead of praising God for his generosity, they cursed him for bringing them out to die in battle.

This was just an echo of their defeatist attitude back in Egypt. At first they believed in Moses, but when Pharaoh refused to release them, they gave up all hope. They "did not listen to Moses, because of their broken spirit and harsh slavery" (Exod. 6:9). For centuries they had been enslaved and that was all they knew. They were the drudges at the bottom of society who did the bidding of their masters. They were hopeless, helpless, worthless.

They had likely also learned yet another kind of "small" thinking from the pagan world around them. The common theology of the polytheistic ancient Near East was that humans were created to be the slaves of gods. Each nation served gods who were finite and limited in power and whose main concern was warfare and gaining power over the other gods. Human beings were their minions, mere pawns in their battles for supremacy. Powerful nations had powerful gods who won their battles. Weak nations had wimpy gods who lost. Every battle was a contest between the gods, and everybody knew who the winners and losers were. Egypt's military prowess was legendary, and its pantheon of terrifying gods towered over the nation from its monumental temples. These colossal structures reminded everyone of Egypt's fearsome protectors.

Puny Nation, Mighty God

You need to "think small" in order to appreciate the impact of Exodus on its original audience. God didn't just thunder a theological pronouncement from the sky in order to reveal himself to the world. He proved himself by duking it out with the mightiest deities they knew. More than once, when Israel approached other nations, the nations reacted in terror at the reputation of this God who had vanquished the Egyptian gods (see Num. 22; Josh. 6). When Moses wanted to remind Israel of the supremacy of their God, he recalled this unparalleled event in history:

> Ask now of the days that are past, which were before you, since the day that God created man on the earth, and ask from one end of heaven to the other, whether such a great thing as this has ever happened. . . . Has any god ever attempted to go and take a nation for himself from the midst of another nation, by trials, by signs, by wonders, and by war, by a mighty hand and an outstretched arm, and by great deeds of terror, all of which the LORD your God did for you in Egypt before your eyes? (Deut. 4:32, 34)

Reading the beginning of Exodus through ancient eyes, you can see how laughable it was for some no-name god to demand that Pharaoh allow the miserable Israelite peons to hold a feast in the wilderness. Pharaoh simply scoffed at this out-of-town, wannabe deity as he ordered his slaves back to work:

> Afterward Moses and Aaron went and said to Pharaoh, "Thus says the Lord, the God of Israel, 'Let my people go, that they may hold a feast to me in the wilderness.'" But Pharaoh said, "Who is the Lord, that I should obey his voice and let Israel go? I do not know the Lord, and moreover, I will not let Israel go." Then they said, "The God of the Hebrews has met with us. Please let us go a three days' journey into the wilderness that we may sacrifice to the Lord our God, lest he fall upon us with pestilence or with the sword." But the king of Egypt said to them, "Moses and Aaron, why do you take the people away from their work? Get back to your burdens." (Exod. 5:1–4)

As the Exodus story unfolds, God makes known to everyone his true power—both the Egyptians and Israelites. As this unknown deity approaches, the plagues on Egypt become increasingly worse. First the river runs red from a distant danger sweeping downstream, then the insects start swarming, then the animals start dying. Then the sky grows ever blacker with hail, locusts, and utter darkness as this awesome God draws near.

Finally, when the Israelites go ahead and sacrifice a lamb and worship their God right in Egypt, his power is unleashed on the Egyptians, and destruction is poured out on Israel's oppressors. Because Pharaoh would not release Israel to worship their God, he had come to punish their captors and release them himself.

We utterly miss the point when we "think big" and wonder why an infinite God needs to demonstrate himself through such primitive, violent imagery. Why didn't he just teleport the Israelites to the promised land in an instant? Why couldn't he just send Christ right then, and explain his nature in modern theological terms? Each of the plagues was, in fact, a theological statement. Each was an assault on one of the terrifying gods of Egypt, showing the deity's impotence compared to that of Israel's God.[7] God was revealing himself in the language that the ancient Near Eastern world understood, not that of modern Westerners.

The idea that God was pretending to be "small" seems to be woven into the details of the story itself. The two miracles that God gave Moses to demonstrate to Pharoah, the staff that changed into a snake and the leprous hand, were both ones that the magicians could reproduce, at least in part (7:20–24). The first two plagues they could replicate too (8:1–14). The third plague, a seemingly mild one where dust is turned to gnats, was when the magicians started to sweat. This, they declared, was the finger of God—none of their gods could create life!

It's like God was deliberately tossing the Egyptians a few lowballs in order to heighten the drama. God was playing the part of a mousy, wimpy Clark Kent who strolls into a seedy saloon and challenges the toughest thugs in town to a brawl. First he pushes up his horn-rimmed glasses, pulls a card deck out of his pocket protector, and does a cheesy trick. The bad guys just snicker and guffaw as they swill their beer. But then Clark starts loosening his tie and taking off his glasses, and everyone knows what will happen next . . .

Regaining a Sense of Awe

How can we regain a sense of awe for God? We can certainly read the psalms and meditate on this biblical way of looking at the world. The next thing we can do is pray, which at its heart is an admission of our smallness. Indeed, praying is an *enactment* of smallness, of assuming that we are not sufficient in ourselves and that a loving God is present and listening to our worries and concerns.

Christians can learn from a Jewish style of prayer that goes back to the time of Christ, that of "blessing the Lord" for every good thing. For millennia, the tradition has been to pepper one's day with numerous short prayers of praise to God in response to each good thing we encounter around us.

For example, when you hear thunder, you say, "Blessed are you, Lord our God, King of the universe, whose strength and power fill the world."

When you put on a new piece of clothing for the first time, you pray, "Blessed are you, Lord our God, King of the universe, who clothes the naked."

When you peel an orange, you say, "Blessed are you . . . who gives a pleasant smell to fruit."

It's impossible to not feel a sense of awe and gratitude when you continually remind yourself of God's presence and loving care. Paul tells us to "pray continually, give thanks in all circumstances" (1 Thess. 5:17–18 NIV). Likely this habit of prayer was in the back of his mind as he said this.[8]

Notice that these prayers go even beyond thanking God for things in our lives. Certainly we can say "thank you" for a fragrant, tasty orange we've just enjoyed. But the form of the traditional prayer focuses on praising God as the source of all blessing and leaves out "me" entirely. All the focus is on God and the good things he has done—not just for me, but for everyone.

What Is Man That You Are Mindful of Him?

In the ancient Near East, it was assumed that humanity was created to be the slaves of gods who were capricious and not terribly interested in their lives. As they saw it, the world was arbitrary, unpredictable, and cruel, and humans had no guarantee that their lives were meaningful in any way. The writing of ancient Mesopotamia betrays a perpetual sense of anxiety because of the helplessness of humanity in their clutches. Humans had no hope of anything beyond survival in a callous, unpredictable world.

Until we grasp this ingrained sense of insignificance, we can't appreciate how stunning the thought was that lowly humankind is somehow precious to God and of intimate concern to him:

> When I look at your heavens, the work of your fingers,
> the moon and the stars, which you have set in place,
> what is man that you are mindful of him,
> and the son of man that you care for him?
> Yet you have made him a little lower than the heavenly beings
> and crowned him with glory and honor.
> (Ps. 8:3–5)

The fact that God has crowned us with glory has not changed the fact that we are "little." We might be small, but God created us to reflect his holy image to creation. This is the ultimate source of human dignity and the reason that human life is precious to God.

According to Nahum Sarna, the idea that humanity is precious to God was actually a prominent, startling theme in the Torah to its original audience in Moses' time. It begins with a creation account that deliberately contradicts pagan myths. Instead of bloody tales of gods waging battles and chopping each other into bits to create the world, Genesis tells the story of the creation of humanity, who is created to be God's image-bearer and appointed to reign over the world.[9] We humans may be tiny, but we are exceedingly precious to God.

A Radical Idea in the Torah

As a whole, human life was incredibly cheap in ancient times, and Near Eastern law codes reflected this fact. Imagine this scenario: a man is leading his ox across a river when he is attacked and murdered by another man, who steals the ox. What's the penalty? Among the Hittites, the murderer would be expected to join the victim's clan and do the work the victim was doing. The actual loss of life meant nothing.

Similarly, in the ancient world, murder was considered a debt between two clans that could be paid off with a sum of money. Or, in some law codes, the murderer could give one of the people they "owned" in exchange, like a wife, a son, or a slave. Or even a few camels, sheep, or cows.

According to renowned scholar Moshe Greenberg, this is where the laws of Israel fundamentally diverged from those of other nations.[10] Many of Israel's distinctive laws were based on the peculiar and supreme value that God placed on human life. Unlike anywhere else, in Israel, murder was seen as an offense against God himself. Because humans were created in the image of God, they bore immense value to him. No amount of money could be exchanged for a life, because nothing could compensate for murder except for the life of the murderer himself.

> "Whoever sheds the blood of man,
> by man shall his blood be shed,
> for God made man in his own image." (Gen. 9:6)

Notice that in biblical thinking, capital punishment is not the same as murder. One is wanton, malicious violence, the other is a penalty demanded by God for a heinous crime. Humanity is precious to God, but human life is not so supreme that even justice cannot demand it. God gave human beings life, and he has the final say in how much life each one of us is given. If we destroy others, he can demand our life back if he wants.[11]

The idea that human life was uniquely precious to God was radical, unparalleled. To us it is second nature, but this was a shocking notion in the world of the ancient Near East. The sanctity of human life is such a part of the bedrock of our thinking that we can hardly imagine a world without it. Our society and our laws have been utterly transformed by it. We just don't realize how novel this was in its ancient setting.

Even in Genesis we find a startling message. We discover that human beings were lovingly fashioned by God and precious to him, and yet they were plagued by sin. As grieved as God was, he committed himself to find another answer to the problem of evil than simply to destroy sinners. Already, we are hearing the embryonic essence of the future redemption of sinners by Christ.

TOOLS AND REFLECTIONS

Reading

Early in the morning, or at the end of a peaceful day, go outside and find yourself a lovely, quiet place to sit. Read some of the passages below out loud.

1. First, imagine yourself as an ancient Israelite who has just been freed from slavery in Egypt and who witnessed the parting of the Red Sea with your own two eyes. Then read the Song of Moses in Exodus 15:1–18 as if you were there. What do you feel?

2. Now, imagine you lived in Jerusalem in King Solomon's time and are standing in front of the just-completed temple. Read the story of Solomon's dedication from 2 Chronicles 5–6, reimagining the scene.

3. Read Psalm 103, imagining that you're hearing King David himself singing about how weak and small he and Israel are, and how great God's love is in comparison.

4. Meditate on Psalm 104, letting yourself picture the imagery of the natural world from the perspective of a person in biblical times. Just try to *be there*. Remember that God loved and spoke to worshipers for millennia before science was on people's minds. What is most awe-inspiring in this psalm?

Thoughts for Going Deeper

- Check out the following books:

  Abraham Joshua Heschel, *The Sabbath* (New York: Farrar, Straus and Giroux, 1951). An outstanding book on the Sabbath, about how ceasing for a day helps us to regain a sense of awe of God.

  Nahum Sarna, *Understanding Genesis* (New York: Schocken Books, 1966). A classic work on the uniqueness of Genesis in light of its original, ancient context.

- You may also enjoy the chapter "For Everything a Blessing" in my book *Sitting at the Feet of Rabbi Jesus* (pages 91–100). Try out this prayerful attitude where a person blesses the Lord for every good thing.

PART 3

Reading about the Messiah

Seeing Him through Hebrew Eyes

9

Memory Is Critical

Hinting at the Scriptures

As Jesus and the other disciples strode along the limestone pavers of the Emmaus road, the dappled sunlight waned. Nobody noticed the sun drop lower and lower in the sky, so intense was the discussion. Jesus was leading the group on a mental hike through the Scriptures: Genesis, Deuteronomy, Isaiah, Psalms, Hosea, and Malachi. If I were trailing behind them, trying to overhear this conversation of the ages, I would have had to pull out a smartphone to hunt up references on my electronic Bible. Beneath the folds of my robe I would have been discreetly tapping away at lightning speed, just trying to keep up.

How can a person study the Bible without a text in front of them? Not many years ago, scholars asked a similar question about Paul. His letters are studded with allusions and subtle Scripture references. Hardly a paragraph goes by without hints and quotations from his Bible. Scholars wondered how he did it. Did he haul a cartful of scrolls from town to town? Did he stop by the synagogue in each village, spending evenings scouring their scroll collection by lamplight for his next sermon?

Ed Sanders, a well-known New Testament scholar, formed a theory based on his own childhood experiences. As a kid he liked to learn epic poems from his mother's English textbooks by memory. He especially liked the ones with blood and gore, fast-paced action, and great rhythm, like the "The Midnight Ride of Paul Revere," which he learned for his tenth birthday, just for the fun of it.

Sanders's schoolteachers were disdainful of this waste of his mental abilities. They chided him that rote memorization would ruin creativity and squash his intellectual growth. He still remembered the day when his teacher lectured the class, "Students should not memorize, but just know where to look things up."

Five decades later, Sanders thought back to the poems he had learned as a kid and noticed that learning them by memory gave him the ability to do many of the things that Paul did. He could still recite lengthy texts with little deviation from the original. If two passages were similar, he would associate them with each other. He could quickly recall verses containing an interesting word and do a mental word study, comparing the passages that shared the word in common.

At conferences, Sanders shared his theory that Paul must have learned his Scriptures by memory. That was how he was able to link passages without spending hours in research, laboring over scroll after scroll, which had no indexes or chapter markings. From audience to audience, Sanders got the same response from Christian scholars:

"Highly unlikely."
"Totally impossible."

Whenever he had Jewish scholars in the room, however, they'd all nod in agreementwith his theory. They knew that far more memorization than just the Bible has been expected in Orthodox Jewish education down through the centuries. Traditionally, boys have studied the Hebrew Bible in school until about age ten, and then a commentary on the Torah called the *Mishnah* (200 AD) in the early preteen years. Then comes *Talmud* study, which stretches into adulthood. The Talmud is an encyclopedic expansion of the discussions in the Mishnah, more than twenty volumes written between 400–500 AD.

One of the Jewish scholars asked Sanders afterward, "What else do you think Paul knew?" The Mishnah records sayings between 200 BC and 200 AD and mentions Paul's own teacher, Gamaliel, in dozens of places. Of course Paul knew his Bible, but how much of the Mishnah and other material might he have known?[1]

If you read rabbinic sermons, you'll find them bubbling over with quotations and allusions to the Scriptures, just like Sanders had noticed in Paul's writing. Historian Martin Jaffee comments,

> We cannot read the surviving Rabbinic literature at all without encountering the sages' stunning ability to summon

> apparently obscure scriptural texts as rhetorical testimonial to various points of Rabbinic law and theology. This mastery of the scriptural text testifies to a comprehensive project of memorization that yielded a scripture known backwards and forwards, inside out and upside down. . . . The mind-stopping display of scriptural erudition obvious in nearly any Rabbinic exegetical discourse on scripture reminds us that the sages knew their scripture with a physical intimacy reminiscent of the Hebrew double entendre regarding the word "knowledge" (*da'at*). Scripture was first and foremost known through a possession as intimate as the taste in one's mouth, encountered textually as a presence lodged in memory and brought to expression in the tongue's speech. In this crucial sense, the written Torah was an oral as much as a written text, a possession within the body as much as a material object in the world.[2]

Learning by Memory

As shocking as the approach of learning by rote seems to us, this kind of education was not unlike that of the rest of antiquity. The cultural elite of the Greeks memorized the works of poets and philosophers and the Romans learned Latin material. The poetry they passed down wasn't just stories, legends, and love ballads. Rather, the great oral works of poetry served as a "massive repository of useful knowledge, a sort of encyclopedia of ethics, politics, history and technology which the effective citizen was required to learn as the core of his educational equipment."[3] Before the widespread use of writing, knowledge was not stored on bookshelves but rather in brains. To be educated was to have an encyclopedic recall of the words of great thinkers.

Around the first century, a system of formal schooling for Jewish boys began in the synagogue. (Some ancient witnesses record this as happening in the first century BC, some in the first century AD.) That was likely where Jesus learned to read, as we see him doing in Luke 4. In the schoolroom, learning was largely by memory. Historian Shmuel Safrai comments:

> Individual and group study of the Bible, repetition of the passages, etc., were often done by chanting them aloud. There is the frequent expression, "the chirping of children," which was heard by people passing close by a synagogue as the children were reciting a verse.[4]

It was also typical for boys to repeat their lessons as they strolled along the dusty roads, something seen in Arab villages even now. You can hear their passion for learning by memory in this saying:

> A person who repeats his lesson a hundred times is not to be compared with him who repeats it a hundred and one times![5]

Synagogue and Supper Table

What about girls and others who might not have gone to school? Two more opportunities would have given them quite a bit of exposure to the Scriptures. The Torah and Prophets were read aloud and preached on in the synagogue for hours each Sabbath. One of the elders of the community (or a visiting teacher) would read the passages and then teach the congregation from them.

Along with the weekly reading in the synagogue was a tradition of always having a discussion of the Scriptures at festive gatherings. This is called a *davar torah* (dah-VAHR to-RAH), a word of teaching. Each week on Friday night, after a family celebrated the Sabbath with the best meal of the week, the father would share a lesson from the passage currently being studied in the synagogue. At holiday gatherings and family celebrations this was the practice too. Safrai writes:

> Torah study was a remarkable feature in Jewish life at the time of the Second Temple and during the period following it. It was not restricted to the formal setting of schools and synagogue, nor to sages only, but became an integral part of ordinary Jewish life. The Torah was studied at all possible times, even if only a little at a time. . . . The sound of Torah learning issuing from houses at night was a common phenomenon. When people assembled for a joyous occasion such as a circumcision or a wedding, a group might withdraw to engage in study of the Law.[6]

Jesus lived in a culture steeped in Bible study, which emphasized the importance of discussing the Scriptures at mealtime by saying, "When three eat at one table and words of Torah are not spoken there, it is as if they ate at the altars of the dead . . . but when three eat at one table and bring up words of Torah, it is as if they ate from the table of God!" (Mishnah, Avot 3:4).[7] Something about the study of God's Word invokes his presence and makes the gathering holy.

Did Paul and Jesus follow this tradition? It's not unlikely. We see many times when the early church gathered to eat and learn from Paul. We often find Jesus teaching at the banquet table too. Jesus was likely welcomed to many a meal because people wanted to hear him expound on the Scriptures.

Christian scholars have scratched their heads over Paul's reasoning in his argument against teachers who forbid certain foods in 1 Timothy 4:

> For everything created by God is good, and nothing is to be rejected if it is received with gratitude; for it is sanctified by means of the word of God and prayer. (vv. 4–5 NASB)

What did Paul mean about the food being sanctified by the "word of God and prayer"? Could he have been thinking of the tradition of sharing a *davar torah* at mealtime that invokes God's presence and sanctifies the gathering, as other Jewish teachers did?

Note also that an enormous amount of knowledge could be gained over years of listening, even if a person had never gone to school or learned to read. Literacy was not required to be very knowledgeable in the Scriptures. Notice that both the synagogue and supper table were equal-opportunity forums for learners—both boys and girls would have had ample opportunity to hear the Scriptures read and discussed. Even though there were no women who were known as rabbinic teachers, some women participated in advanced forums in the synagogue and contributed opinions that became authoritative in rabbinic law.

When I first heard about the memory that Jesus' Jewish culture had for its Scriptures, I was skeptical too. Part of my skepticism, I think, was that I envisioned memory solely as the ability to recite a monologue without prompting. Certainly the most highly trained teachers could rattle off entire books of the Bible.[8] Jewish practice, however, was to always study in a group, so that the memory skill that was important for participants to have was the ability to mentally locate a text in a wider context, not recite an entire book by rote. I imagine this was the skillset of men and women who didn't get a formal education. Some were more skilled and some less, but still better than we are today.

Indeed, this was even true in the church in former centuries. C. S. Lewis points out that the King James Version became widely familiar to people after it was published in 1611:

> For three centuries the Bible was so well known that hardly any word or phrase, except those which it shared with all English books whatever, could be borrowed without recognition. If you echoed the Bible everyone knew that you were echoing the Bible. And certain associations were called up in every reader's mind—sacred associations. All your readers had heard it read, as a ritual or almost ritual act, at home, at school, and in church. . . . There could be a pious use and a profane use: but there could be no ordinary use.[9]

Preachers over the ages could allude to a verse and expect listeners to catch their reference. When Martin Luther King Jr. gave his "I Have a Dream" speech, he could preach that "we will not be satisfied until *justice rolls down like waters, and righteousness like a mighty stream*" (Amos 5:24) and expect listeners to hear the rebuke of the prophet Amos rumbling through his words. Words of Scripture added authority to King's sermon, inferring that God himself was outraged by the racial injustice of America in the 1960s.

"Hinting" at the Scriptures

What Martin Luther King Jr. did, Jesus and Paul did—and on an even more sophisticated level. It was not uncommon for rabbis to "hint" to the Bible with only a word or two and expect listeners to recall a whole passage. Sometimes the reference could be quite important for getting their point.[10] Here's one passage where Jesus uses this technique:

> He entered the temple and began to drive out those who sold, saying to them, "It is written, 'My house shall be a house of prayer,' but you have made it a den of robbers." (Luke 19:45–46)

On the surface, Jesus' words sound quite tepid, as if he was outlawing monetary transactions during worship. Was he voicing an objection to church coffee bars that charge money for lattes on Sunday mornings?

If you know his references, you'll see that Jesus' rebuke of the money changers was packed with far more punch. He was contrasting two famous prophecies about the temple. The first came from Isaiah's glorious vision of universal worship in chapter 56:

> The foreigners who join themselves to the Lord,
> to minister to him, to love the name of the Lord,
> and to be his servants . . .
> these I will bring to my holy mountain,
> and make them joyful in my house of prayer;
> their burnt offerings and their sacrifices
> will be accepted on my altar;
> for my *house shall be called a house of prayer*
> for all peoples. (Isa. 56:6–7, emphasis added)

This passage describes God's greatest promise for the temple, that it would be a place where God would be worshiped by the whole world.

The second prophecy Jesus referenced, however, came from Jeremiah's judgment of the temple of his day because of its corruption:

> Will you steal, murder, commit adultery, swear falsely, make offerings to Baal, and go after other gods that you have not known, and then come and stand before me in this house, which is called by my name, and say, "We are delivered!"—only to go on doing all these abominations? Has this house, which is called by my name, become a *den of robbers* in your eyes? Behold, I myself have seen it, declares the LORD. Go now to my place that was in Shiloh, where I made my name dwell at first, and see what I did to it because of the evil of my people Israel. (Jer. 7:9–12, emphasis added)

The Jeremiah passage describes the temple's worst possible abuse, where people committed wicked acts openly and then fled to the temple believing that God would protect it from destruction. God had let the tabernacle at Shiloh be destroyed, Jeremiah warned, and he'd do the same again.

Once you hear the contrast between these two prophecies, Jesus' words in Mark 11 overflow with rebuke. Jesus was assaulting the money-changing tables, which were called the "booths of Annas" because they were owned by the family of the high priest Annas (or Ananias). It's historically known that the house of Annas charged greatly inflated prices on sacrificial animals, extorted money, and stole funds intended for priests who had no other income. Heard in its full context, Mark 11 expands into a prophecy about the destruction of the temple because of priestly corruption. Seen in this light, it fits with Jesus' other words of condemnation during Passion Week.

Jesus was likely linking the two passages because they contained the same distinctive Hebrew word or phrase, "my house."[11] This technique was called *gezerah shava* (geh-zer-AH sha-VAH), "a comparison of equals." As you can imagine, it took an excellent recall of the Scriptures to mentally match two passages with a unique word.

We find another example of this technique in Jesus' answer to the query about which of the commandments is the greatest:

> The most important is, "Hear, O Israel: The Lord our God, the Lord is one. And you shall love the Lord your God with all your heart and with all your soul and with all your mind and with all your strength." The second is this: "You shall love your neighbor as yourself." There is no other commandment greater than these. (Mark 12:29–31)

Jesus was quoting from two passages from the Torah, Deuteronomy 6:4–5 and Leviticus 19:18. Both of these lines share a distinctive word, *v'ahavta* (ve-ah-HAV-tah, "and you shall love"), so Jewish teachers would meditate on how the two lines might reflect on each other:

> You shall love the Lord your God with all your heart. (Deut. 6:5)

> You shall love your neighbor as yourself. (Lev. 19:18)

The second is like the first, Jesus declared. Indeed, it could even be said that in order to love the Lord your God with all of your heart, you need to love your neighbor as yourself.

As sophisticated as this seems, other rabbinic teachers would not just match one or two references but several, deliberately linking together passage after passage. This practice, called "stringing pearls," forced the audience to listen attentively and quickly leapfrog across Scripture in order to catch the preacher's point.[12] Truly, Israel's sages were masters of memory.

A Kind of Alzheimer's

Much of the reason we've found Jesus' words so hard to grasp is because we are so unfamiliar with the Scriptures he loved—the Torah, the Prophets, and the Writings. Sandra Richter calls the church's lack of memory of Israel's Scriptures a kind of Alzheimer's disease. She writes:

> The church's lack of knowledge of their own heritage renders much of the wealth of the New Testament inaccessible to them. . . . I realize that this is a painful metaphor for many of us, but it is, unfortunately, appropriate. The great tragedy of Alzheimer's disease is that it robs a person of themselves by robbing them of their memory of their experiences and relationships. Hence, an elderly woman with Alzheimer's can watch her own children walk through the door and need to ask their names. (As a mother, I cannot imagine the agony of such a state.) The church has a similar condition. Just as the Alzheimer's patient must ask the name of her own children, the church watches her ancestors walk through the door with a similar response. Abraham, Isaac and Jacob are unknown and unnamed. The end result: The church does not know who she is, because she does not know who she was.[13]

How do we remedy this? By seriously engaging with the Old Testament for itself and not just to mine for prooftexts and predictions of Christ. By loving the family of our Lord by opening our ears to hear their epic story, and then joyfully listening to its echoes in the New Testament. We'll look a little more at this in these final chapters.

TOOLS AND REFLECTIONS

Reading

1. During Jesus' triumphal entry into Jerusalem on the donkey, immediately before he clears the temple, his words in Luke 19:37–44 are filled with allusions to his Scriptures. Look up the following passages and read a few verses surrounding them to get a sense for their wider context. (It helps to use a more "word-for-word" translation like the KJV, ESV, or NASB to catch the words they have in common.) How does knowing Jesus' reference expand your understanding of the scene in Luke?

   Luke 19:40—Habakkuk 2:11

   Luke 19:42—Isaiah 59:8

   Luke 19:43—Isaiah 29:3

   The crowd quotes Psalm 118:26—what do they say?

2. A little later in the temple, in Luke 20:17, Jesus quotes a line, "The stone that the builders rejected has become the cornerstone," which comes from Psalm 118:22. This psalm was seen as messianic because kings and leaders were spoken of as "cornerstones." Read the psalm and see how it fits the triumphal entry scene.

   After the "cornerstone" quotation, what was Jesus' next line in Luke 20:18? Read Isaiah 8:14–15. How do Jesus' words relate?

How about the dream that Daniel interprets in Daniel 2:31–35?

How does all the "stone" imagery in Psalm 118, Isaiah 8, and Daniel 2 deepen your understanding of Jesus' words?

Thoughts for Going Deeper

- Consider committing passages, even books, to memory and sharing them with others as part of your studies.
- Personally, I've found that listening to the Scriptures read aloud is sometimes better than reading them on a page, especially for learning by memory. Whenever I study with others, we always read aloud. It seems like the Spirit speaks especially loudly when God's Word becomes our words. If you don't have a human nearby, many apps are available that you can use to play an audio Bible aloud as you commute or exercise.
- For more on Jesus' habit of "hinting," read "Stringing Pearls" in *Sitting at the Feet of Rabbi Jesus*, 36–49.
- A very useful volume for studying Jesus' allusions is G. K. Beale and D. A. Carson, *Commentary on the New Testament Use of the Old Testament* (Grand Rapids: Baker Academic, 2007).

10

Moses and the Prophets Have Spoken

Finding Promises in the Synagogue

As Luke parts the curtains on Jesus' public ministry, we find him reading from Isaiah in a Sabbath service in the synagogue of Nazareth in Luke 4. Participating in this gathering of prayer and Scripture reading, Luke explains, has been Jesus' lifelong weekly habit, and it will become a common backdrop of his ministry. Paul, too, will aim his outreach at the synagogue. The Scriptures were front and center there, and that was where the common people came to hear the Bible read and preached.

What can we know about the synagogue environment of their ministries? You might be surprised at how many clues we can gather about that scene.

In Acts 13:15 we read that Paul was invited to address the congregation after the public reading of the Law (Torah) and the Prophets (Neviim). If you've ever visited a modern synagogue, you know that this tradition continues to this day. For more than two millennia, "the Law and the Prophets" have been the centerpiece of the synagogue reading liturgy, even until today.

For centuries, traditional Jewish practice has been to read the entire Torah aloud each year. Selections from the Neviim (which include both prophetic writings and historical books) are also read that fit the theme of the Torah reading. The Torah portion is called the *parashah* (par-a-SHAH, pl. *parashot*; par-a-SHOTE), and the reading from the Neviim is called the *haftarah* (haf-ta-RAH, pl. *haftarot*; haf-ta-ROTE), which means "completion." After the prophetic reading, a sermon or homily is shared that is based on the passages. If you grew up in a liturgical tradition like I did, you'll recognize the habit of reading the Bible aloud, passage by passage, week by week. Christians inherited this practice from the ancient synagogue.

Across the world, every synagogue reads the same text each week, so that anywhere you go, the same Bible passage is on the minds of Jews everywhere. This rhythmic pattern is so engrained in Jewish life that even secular Israeli calendars mark off the weeks of the year by the names of the *parashah* that will be read that week. Can you imagine participating in a Bible study so universal that you can glance at a free calendar you got at the bank to see what you'll be studying this week?

In Orthodox synagogues, the same Scripture texts have been recited each week of the year for over fifteen centuries.[1]

On the day they finish reading Deuteronomy, they throw a big party that they call *Simchat Torah* (sim-KHAHT to-RAH)—"The Joy of the Torah." After parading the scrolls around the synagogue with great pomp and circumstance, they read the last word of Deuteronomy followed immediately by the first words of Genesis. Not a moment should be spent outside of the Scriptures. A well-known saying epitomizes their feelings:

> Turn it, and turn it, for everything is in it. Reflect on it and grow old and gray with it. Don't turn from it, for nothing is better than it.[2]

Evidence of Older Synagogue Tradition

The tradition of reading through the Torah annually according to a standardized lectionary is indeed ancient, dating back to 400–500 AD. In the Babylonian Talmud that was written about 500 AD, it is assumed to be the practice. Earlier Jewish writings do not refer to this practice, however, so the custom before 500 AD remained a mystery until about a century ago.

You've heard of the discovery of the Dead Sea Scrolls in 1946, but you may never have heard of another momentous discovery of Hebrew texts that occurred fifty years earlier in Cairo, Egypt. In 1896, over three hundred thousand Jewish documents dating back over a thousand years were found in a synagogue *genizah* (geh-NEE-zah), a storeroom for worn-out holy texts.

Among these texts were multiple synagogue lectionary lists. To the amazement of the discoverers, these were not the annual readings they knew so well but were from a more ancient synagogue tradition that had persisted in Israel, northern Africa, and Egypt until at least 1100 AD.[3]

As researchers examined the lists, they could see that the modern Torah-reading liturgy was derived from this older tradition. Instead of splitting the text of the Torah into about fifty readings for study over a year, it was split into about 150–170 readings, likely taking about three and a half years to complete. One ancient traveler from Babylon to Israel remarked that in Israel, synagogues celebrated *Simchat Torah* every three years instead of every one, and different villages celebrated it at different times. This comment, along with the fact that reading lists varied in length, suggested that synagogues weren't synchronized before the annual cycle was instituted in Babylon. Jesus and Paul would have encountered different villages at slightly different places in the text as they traveled and preached.

The most fascinating thing that researchers found was that while the Torah readings had hardly changed, the *haftarah* readings from the Prophets were completely different. In the modern liturgy, readings are chosen from historical narratives and relate the Torah reading to an event in Israel's history. For example,

Torah: Genesis 1 **Haftarah:** Isaiah 42:5–43:10	Creation of the world God is the unique creator of the world
Torah: Genesis 47:28–50:26 **Haftarah:** 1 Kings 2:1–12	Jacob's dying words to his sons King David's dying words to Solomon
Torah: Exodus 13:17–17:16 **Haftarah:** Judges 4:4–5:31	Miriam's song at the Red Sea Deborah's victory song
Torah: Leviticus 12:1–13:59 **Haftarah:** 2 Kings 4:42–5:19	Purification after childbirth and skin disease Healing of Naaman from leprosy

In the earlier triennial tradition, the interest was not in Israel's past but in Israel's future. There, the *haftarah* readings focused on God's promises of a glorious future kingdom and a coming messianic age. Every week in the synagogue, the readings asked: What would the world look like when God established his kingdom on earth? How would the story of Israel play out in his ultimate plan?

During the week they'd meditate on the creation story in Genesis 1, they'd also read about the new creation in Isaiah 65:

> "For behold, I create new heavens
>   and a new earth,
> and the former things shall not be remembered
>   or come into mind. . . .
> The wolf and the lamb shall graze together;
>   the lion shall eat straw like the ox,
>   and dust shall be the serpent's food.
> They shall not hurt or destroy
>   in all my holy mountain,"
> says the Lord. (Isa. 65:17, 25)

And on the week that they read about when God confounded the languages at the tower of Babel in Genesis 11, they'd read his promise in Zephaniah 3:9:

> For at that time I will change the speech of the
>   peoples
>   to a pure speech,
> that all of them may call upon the name of the Lord
>   and serve him with one accord.

When they read about Moses descending Mount Sinai with the tablets of the covenant in Exodus 34:27–35, they'd read

Jeremiah 31:32–39, about God making a new covenant with his people:

> This is the covenant that I will make with the house of Israel after those days, declares the LORD: I will put my law within them, and I will write it on their hearts. And I will be their God, and they shall be my people. (Jer. 31:33)

When they read Leviticus 12–13, about purification after childbirth, they'd read Isaiah 9:6:

> For to us a child is born,
> to us a son is given;
> and the government shall be upon his shoulder,
> and his name shall be called
> Wonderful Counselor, Mighty God,
> Everlasting Father, Prince of Peace.

Why? Because the prophetic passage was chosen that would point forward to some promise of God's future redemption. Isaiah 9 contains a vision of the birth of one who would sit on David's throne and have an eternal kingdom. When synagogues read about the regulations for new mothers, they would look forward to the birth of the Messiah.

A Kingdom-Oriented Lectionary

Christians should be fascinated by the fact that the dominant theme of the earliest synagogue lectionaries was God's coming redemption. It fits with Jesus' preaching from town to town that God's kingdom had arrived in his life and ministry.

Especially notable is that over half of the prophetic readings came from Isaiah, especially chapters 40–66, which focus on promises of redemption and renewal.[4] Jesus often quoted Isaiah 40–66. When he read in the synagogue in Luke 4, he was quoting from Isaiah 61, and the Beatitudes in Matthew 5 are filled with references from Isaiah 55–57 and Isaiah 66. Paul's favorite book to quote was also Isaiah.

Do we know what lectionary was used in New Testament times? Scholars believe that while the Torah reading was predetermined, the haftarah passage was left up to the reader. Lectionaries date from later centuries, but they developed out of the reading practices of Jesus' day. Then, the person who read the Torah portion would also select the prophetic portion and deliver a homily. Differently educated synagogue members (or visiting teachers) would take turns each week doing the public reading. It was up to the speaker to choose a *haftarah* that fit the Torah passage and yielded a good sermon.

Choosing a prophetic reading took an impressive amount of biblical knowledge. Besides commenting on the Torah in some clever or profound way, the *haftarah* would also usually begin with a verse that had a key word in common with the beginning of the Torah reading. Then it would end with a promise of future redemption, sometimes skipping verses to end on a happy note.

Take a look at Genesis 1:1: "In the beginning, God created *the heavens and the earth*" (emphasis added). It is echoed by Isaiah 65:17: "Behold, I am creating a new heavens and a new earth" (NJPS). The rest of the passage, Isaiah 65:17–25, describes a vision of a renewed creation where the wolf and the lamb graze together and the cursedness of creation in Genesis is reversed.

For any Torah reading there are a finite number of possible passages in the Prophets to choose from, so certain *haftarah* readings became "magnetized" to passages in the Torah. Over the years, speakers would come back to them again and again, and some of the most popular passages were later formalized into lectionaries. Even though readings didn't become fixed until a few centuries later, many Torah passages became associated with prophetic readings much earlier.

Fascinatingly, these "magnetized" connections occasionally appear in the New Testament, both in the words of Jesus and Paul.[5] For instance, the triennial lectionary pairs the reading of Genesis 16 with Isaiah 54:1–10. Genesis 16 tells the sad story of Sarah's barrenness and plan to bear Abraham a child through Hagar. Isaiah 54:1–10 offers eschatological hope to end Sarah's sorrow:

> "Sing, O barren one, who did not bear;
> break forth into singing and cry aloud,
> you who have not been in labor!
> For the children of the desolate one will be more
> than the children of her who is married," says the
> Lord. (v. 1)

In Galatians 4, we find Paul making the same connection. He starts with the Sarah/Hagar story and then connects it to the prophecy in Isaiah 54 to support his argument about Gentiles being "sons of Abraham." People have often struggled with Paul's reasoning and wondered why he likened Jews to Hagar, Sarah's Egyptian slave. It almost sounds like Paul had acquired an anti-Semitic streak. However, more than one scholar now thinks he was actually being very Jewish, bringing the Genesis 16-Isaiah 54 linkage into his discussion because people had been connecting the two passages in synagogues even before his time.[6]

The Synagogues of Galilee

Intriguingly, scholars note that the triennial lectionary was formed in the Galilee, although a couple of centuries after the time of Christ. The Galilee was a center of sophisticated religious scholarship, and several of the best rabbis in Jewish literature came from there.[7] Their masterful construction of sermons attests to the brilliance of their scholarship and Google-like familiarity with Scripture.

Galilean teachers were not operating through a translation but in the original language of the Hebrew Bible, by the way. They would often choose the *haftarah* by the technique of *gezerah shava*, in which Scripture passages were linked because of their shared distinctive Hebrew wording. This might surprise readers who have heard that an Aramaic translation (*targum*) was studied instead of the Hebrew Bible. Outside of Israel, the Scriptures were often read in a Greek translation called the Septuagint, but Hebrew was always read in Galilean synagogues.[8]

Scholars do not think it's possible to guess what readings Jesus was preaching on. But the very fact that the messianic kingdom was such a prominent theme in liturgies that developed out of that period should be of interest to Christian readers. Evidence suggests that the Torah was being read as if Israel's prophets were its commentators, elaborating on how each detail of the Torah would find fulfillment in the world to come. Jesus likely taught Scripture in this way too. It seems only natural, since he was preaching about the coming of the kingdom of God.

What Happened to Jesus' *Haftarah*?

You might be wondering: What about the messianic prophecies about Jesus? Like being born of a virgin in Isaiah 7:14? And what about Isaiah 61:1–2, which Jesus read about: "The Lord has anointed me"? How about Micah 5:2, about a ruler being born in Bethlehem, or Zechariah 9:9, about Jerusalem's future king entering the city on a donkey? Where do we find these in synagogue lectionaries?

Brace yourselves, but they are nowhere to be found in the annual lectionary that is used now. Bear in mind that the Torah is read aloud in its entirety during synagogue services, but only a subset of the Neviim is read, selected because it complements the Torah reading. In 2004, an Israeli newspaper published an article called "What Happened to Jesus' Haftarah?" where Jewish scholar Hananel Mack examined the lectionary readings.[9] He concluded that the pattern was clear enough to show that it was intentional. Any passage that was quoted in the New Testament as being about Jesus as the Christ was intentionally avoided in synagogue readings.

This in itself should be a lesson to Christians who are studying their Jewish roots. Many of us are shocked by how the church has lost so much rich knowledge because of its hostility toward Judaism. But Judaism did not take this lying down. As Christians were separating Jesus from his Jewish roots, Jews were separating from him too. When Christians read Jewish sources about Jesus, they should not expect their opinions to be neutral.

Could it be just a coincidence that the fourth century AD, when Jewish liturgy began adopting a lectionary that downplayed prophetic promises, was also the era that Christian persecution of the Jews reached a peak during the reign of Constantine? At the same time that Christians were chopping themselves free of their Jewish roots, the synagogue was silencing the prophecies of a coming Messiah.

Messiah, Son of Joseph

Even the triennial reading lists found in the Cairo Geniza appear to be somewhat sanitized.[10] Yet, in examining the readings, we still see signs that even Jews who were not believers in Jesus were reading the Scriptures looking for how the prophets were envisioning the fulfillment of God's ancient promises.

A few readings in the triennial lectionary are quite telling, particularly those from the story of Joseph. As an example, look at Genesis 39:1–6. I'll quote the beginning and the end here.

> Now Joseph had been brought down to Egypt, and Potiphar, an officer of Pharaoh, the captain of the guard, an Egyptian, had bought him from the Ishmaelites who had brought him down there. The LORD was with Joseph, and he became a successful man, and he was in the house of his Egyptian master. . . . Now Joseph was handsome in form and appearance. (vv. 1–2, 6)

The assigned passage from the Prophets is Isaiah 52:3–53:5, recalling the oppression of the Israelites in Egypt, and then God's promise to respond. It begins:

> For thus says the Lord: "You were sold for nothing, and you shall be redeemed without money." For thus says the Lord God: "My people went down at the first into Egypt to sojourn there." (52:3–4)

The first verse of the Isaiah reading ties Joseph's fate with Israel's. Both went down to Egypt and were sold as slaves. But then Isaiah 52:10 goes on to say how God will be roused to respond and paints scenes of the exodus from Egypt, only adding that now God will do something even greater, something that involves a mysterious "Servant" figure who will enter the scene:

> See, my servant will act wisely;
> he will be raised and lifted up and highly exalted.
> Just as there were many who were appalled at him—
> his appearance was so disfigured beyond that of any human being
> and his form marred beyond human likeness—
> so he will sprinkle many nations,
> and kings will shut their mouths because of him.
> For what they were not told, they will see,
> and what they have not heard, they will understand. (vv. 13–15 NIV)

What does this tell us? For centuries, Jewish congregations were reading Joseph's story in light of the Suffering Servant of Isaiah. The short Genesis reading stops with the words that Joseph was "handsome in appearance," deliberately contrasting with Isaiah 52:14, "his appearance was so marred, beyond human semblance, and his form beyond that of the children of mankind."

The Isaiah reading then goes on:

> Surely he has borne our griefs
> and carried our sorrows;
> yet we esteemed him stricken,
> smitten by God, and afflicted.
> But he was pierced for our transgressions;
> he was crushed for our iniquities;
> upon him was the chastisement that brought us peace,
> and with his wounds we are healed. (53:4–5)

In synagogues after the first century, as people read about the Suffering Servant, they were thinking about Joseph. Consider Joseph's own story. His own brothers hated him, planned to kill him, and threw him into a pit. Then they decided to sell him into slavery in Egypt for the money. While he was there, he was falsely accused of rape and imprisoned in a dungeon for twelve years. It was because of his brothers' hateful actions that Joseph went down into the pit, down into Egypt, and down into the dungeon. Yet, after he interpreted Pharaoh's dream, he was put in command over all of Egypt during an extended famine. Joseph's family would have died in the famine if not for his actions. In fact, Joseph not only saved his brothers but many nations. Hmm.

Jewish tradition has always struggled with the fact that the prophets describe visions of both a royal, victorious King who would reign on the throne of David and a Suffering Servant who would atone for the sins of Israel. Various legends existed that there might need to be two Messiahs, one who would die and another who would reign. The one who suffers was often called the "Messiah ben [son of] Joseph," and the one who reigns was called the "Messiah ben David." It looks like the "Messiah ben Joseph" came from reading Isaiah 52–53 in light of this story.

Could these two figures merge into one person? Looking at the lectionary again, a few weeks after synagogues read about Joseph's imprisonment in Egypt, they read about Pharaoh appointing him in command over Egypt in Genesis 41. That passage begins with Pharaoh asking, "Can we find anyone like this man, one in whom is the spirit of God?" (v. 38 NIV). The prophetic reading for this text is Isaiah 11:2–16, which begins:

> The Spirit of the Lord will rest on him—
> the Spirit of wisdom and of understanding,
> the Spirit of counsel and of might,
> the Spirit of the knowledge and fear of the Lord—
> and he will delight in the fear of the Lord.
> (vv. 2–3 NIV)

This is the beginning of Isaiah's glorious vision of a messianic King. Notice that this comes from Isaiah's famous "shoot from the stump of Jesse" prophecy, about a coming Son of David who would reign over a glorious renewed world.

Congregations were reading about Joseph's suffering in light of Isaiah 52–53, and then a few weeks later about his reign over Egypt in light of Isaiah 11. Hmm . . . do you think that even a Messiah who is a "Son of Joseph" could someday reign?

TOOLS AND REFLECTIONS

Reading

1. Read Genesis 1–2:3 along with its traditional triennial *haftarah*, Isaiah 65:17–25. How does the vision of Isaiah

of the "new creation" overlap with and contrast with Genesis 1?

2. Read Genesis 6:9–7:24 along with its triennial *haftarah*, Isaiah 54:9–17. How does the promise of Isaiah to Israel relate to and expand on it? What vision does it have for the messianic age?

3. Read the story of the Tower of Babel in Genesis 11:1–9. Then read the *haftarah*, Zephaniah 3:9–20. How does the prophet reverse imagery of Genesis 11?

4. Read Genesis 16 along with its ancient *haftarah*, Isaiah 54:1–10. Listen to the story of Sarah in Genesis 16 as if Isaiah 54 is giving her a vision of the future.

   (Isaiah's words are actually to Jerusalem after the exile of its inhabitants. Jerusalem is likened to a woman who is mourning for the loss of her children. Sarah is the "mother" of these children too, because centuries earlier God had promised Abraham he would be the father of many nations [Gen. 17:4].)

5. Read Galatians 4:22–28. How does Paul use Genesis 16 and Isaiah 54 in his argument here?

6. Paul sees Christ's victory over death as inaugurating God's "new creation" because Christ now reigns over God's kingdom. We are living in the messianic age right now. How do the prophecies you've read above relate? What remains to be fulfilled?

Thoughts for Going Deeper

- Imagery from the Torah winds through the rest of the Scriptures, both Old and New Testaments. If you've never studied them, you're missing a lot of material that Jesus and other New Testament writers assumed you'd know. Get started, at least, with a good study of Genesis and Deuteronomy. Or consider reading through the Torah with some friends. You can follow the annual tradition if you start in the fall. Calendars and readings are online.

- Advanced readers: Consider forming a group to read the Torah and *haftarah* according to the ancient "triennial" lectionary. Note: this is not for beginners. It will probably take around four years, and many connections are not obvious. It's fascinating, though, if you have the background. See OurRabbiJesus.com for more information.

11

Reading in the Third Dimension

Listening for Echoes in the Text

When people hear the Scriptures read repeatedly, year after year, they get very, very familiar with the stories, down to the finest details. Every little odd turn of a phrase becomes memorable. Distinctive words stand out when they come up again later.

People start to notice themes rippling through the text and hear how earlier events foreshadow later events. They listen to the story of Ruth in light of her family history and see her replaying the scene her foremothers had acted out long ago. They wouldn't just focus on single stories but rather listen for how details echoed through multiple passages.

Here's an example: Noah built an ark, a *tevah*, to save his family from the flood, and Moses' mother placed her son in a *tevah* on the water to save him from death. The word *tevah* is only used in those two narratives. Notice also that both Moses and Noah were redeemers, and both saved their people from being destroyed by water. Many of these linkages are obvious in Hebrew but are lost in translation.[1]

Is it legitimate to study the Bible this way? In the largely oral society where the Old Testament was composed, repetition was used to emphasize meaning. Later events were described in light of earlier ones to emphasize the interconnections. This is one way that oral cultures encoded meaning, and it is much more obvious when you hear stories repeatedly and know each phrase thoroughly.

Let's look at an example of meditating on one detail of the creation account in a "longitudinal" way. Consider Genesis 1:2:

> The Spirit [*ruach*] of God was hovering over the face of the waters.

What significance does this line have? What is the Bible telling us here? Modern readers usually start off by looking at it from a scientific perspective, and they immediately struggle with why "waters" were present at the creation of the universe. For thousands of years, though, readers of the Bible were entirely unconcerned about this discussion.[2]

Let's consider the perspective of first-century readers. How would they have tried to understand this verse where the Spirit of God is hovering over primeval waters?

What they would do to understand this imagery is listen for when it echoes through the biblical text later on. They would study it longitudinally through the Scriptures. Because the Hebrew word *ruach* means both "Spirit" and "wind," Genesis 8:1 would quickly come to mind:

> God remembered Noah and all the beasts and all the livestock that were with him in the ark. And God made a wind [*ruach*] blow over the earth, and the waters subsided.

Notice that once again God's wind/Spirit is blowing over the waters. More than one rabbi has noted that this replay of the first creation scene is telling us how God was, in effect, creating the world anew after the flood. The waters of the deep in the creation scene gushed forth during the flood to cleanse the land of the bloodshed that had cursed it because of murderous humankind. The "wind" of God blew over the waters and created the world again.

Another place we find God blowing a wind over the waters is at the parting of the Red Sea:

> Then Moses stretched out his hand over the sea, and the LORD drove the sea back by a strong east wind all night and made the sea dry land, and the waters were divided. (Exod. 14:21)

Once again, God is creating, but now this is the creation of the nation of Israel. This was the pinnacle moment, when the Israelites were miraculously liberated from Egypt. The psalms often celebrated this momentous scene at the founding of their nation (Ps. 78:13, for example). Notice that this scene also includes the idea of judgment by water, similar to the flood. While God's enemies are destroyed by water, his people escape unharmed.

The Spirit of the Messiah

Jewish readers also noticed the presence of God's *ruach* in other places, not on waters but on a person. Whenever

God appointed a leader over Israel, he filled him with his *ruach*, his Spirit. Of David it says, "Then Samuel took the horn of oil and anointed him in the midst of his brothers. And the Spirit of the Lord rushed upon David from that day forward" (1 Sam. 16:13). This is true for Saul, too, who surprised everyone by momentarily prophesying (10:10). We find the same scene over and over, with judges like Gideon, Jepthah, and Samson too. When Moses appointed seventy elders to assist him in leading Israel, the text says,

> Then the Lord came down in the cloud and spoke to him, and took some of the Spirit that was on him and put it on the seventy elders. And as soon as the Spirit rested on them, they prophesied. But they did not continue doing it. (Num. 11:25)

God's Spirit seems to be a requisite for every leader. Knowing this sheds light on Isaiah's prophecy about the Messiah, the "branch" from David's tree:

> There shall come forth a shoot from the stump of
> Jesse,
> and a branch from his roots shall bear fruit.
> And the Spirit of the Lord shall rest upon him,
> the Spirit of wisdom and understanding,
> the Spirit of counsel and might,
> the Spirit of knowledge and the fear of the Lord.
> (Isa. 11:1–2)

The prophet Isaiah proclaimed that the King upon whom God's Spirit would rest in a supreme way was the Messiah. He would not just prophesy momentarily but would overflow with supernatural knowledge, understanding, and wise counsel. Most importantly, he would be full of reverence and devotion for the Lord. Doesn't this sound like Christ?

Interestingly, one rabbi connected the scene of creation to this passage. An early rabbinic commentary on Genesis says, "'The Spirit of God hovered . . .' this alludes to 'the Spirit of the Lord shall rest upon him.'"[3] The same Spirit of God that hovered over creation would rest upon the Messiah. Part of this thinking comes from recalling a frequent promise God made about redemption, that he would create "a new heaven and a new earth." The Messiah will reign in glory in this new creation, so it makes sense that the *ruach* that blew over the primeval waters would be the *ruach* Isaiah envisioned resting on the Messiah.

The Hovering Spirit

More than one rabbinic sage noted that the *ruach* of God *hovered* over the waters. You would think that a wind would blow like a breeze from here to there, not hover. The verb that is translated "hovered," *merahefet*, is somewhat unusual. It means to "flutter" or "hover," like a bird flapping its wings. At the creation God's Spirit does not blow, it "flutters" over the waters, like an eagle hovering watchfully over its brood.

> Like an eagle that stirs up its nest,
> that *flutters* over its young,
> spreading out its wings, catching them,
> bearing them on its pinions,
> the LORD alone guided [Israel],
> no foreign god was with him. (Deut. 32:11–12, emphasis added)

When you're aware of the avian imagery, it's hard not to think of another scene of God's *ruach* fluttering over water, when Jesus is baptized in the river Jordan. But now, this time God's *ruach* alights on Jesus like a dove. The Holy Spirit that had hovered over creation had now come to rest on Christ, God's anointed King.

> As soon as Jesus was baptized, he went up out of the water. At that moment heaven was opened, and he saw the Spirit of God descending like a dove and alighting on him. And a voice from heaven said, "This is my Son, whom I love; with him I am well pleased." (Matt. 3:16–17 NIV)

Before, God had created Adam, filled him with the breath of life, and then pronounced this final creation of his "very good." Now, as the Spirit descends on Jesus, God voices his pleasure, "This is my beloved Son, with whom I am well pleased."

On the Third Day . . .

This habit of interpreting the Bible by listening for repeating echoes may shed light on something that Jesus said along the road to Emmaus. Consider a rabbinic comment on a well-known promise of redemption in Hosea:

> Come, let us return to the LORD;
> for he has torn us, that he may heal us;
> he has struck us down, and he will bind us up.
> After two days he will revive us;
> *on the third day he will raise us up*,
> that we may live before him. (Hos. 6:1–2, emphasis added)

Hosea had rebuked the people of Israel for their sins, and they knew they were suffering from God's punishment. But then Hosea invited them to return to the Lord, issuing a gracious promise that God's forgiveness and healing would soon come. This message gave them hope that even when God was angry, he desired to forgive. Today might be a terrible day of his anger, but tomorrow would be better, and in not too long, life would seemingly begin again.

When the rabbis meditated on the Scriptures in light of Hosea's words, they noticed many places where "the third day" was when redemption came.

- When Abraham obeyed God's command to offer up Isaac, the text says that "On the third day Abraham lifted up his eyes" (Gen. 22:4).
- When God called Israel on Mount Sinai, he appeared "On the morning of the third day" (Exod. 19:16).
- After Joseph had imprisoned his brothers, "On the third day [he] said to them, 'Do this and you will live'" (Gen. 42:18).
- Jonah was in the fish's belly "three days and three nights" before he was saved (Jon. 1:17).

Their comment was, "The Holy One, blessed be his name, never lets the just stay in affliction longer than three days."[4] The rabbis were not being woodenly literalistic in actually counting up days. They were not developing codes and prediction schemes. They were saying that scripturally, redemption often comes "on the third day." Jewish scholar Pinchas Lapide writes that in Jewish thought,

> "On the third day" has nothing to do with the date or the counting of time but contains for ears which are educated biblically a clear reference to God's mercy and grace which is revealed after two days of affliction and death by way of redemption.[5]

Lapide believes that this sheds light on Jesus' words in Luke 24:46, "Thus it is written, that the Christ should suffer and on the third day rise from the dead." This line is not specifically found written out verbatim anywhere in the Hebrew Bible. But everybody knew that the Scriptures were permeated with Hosea's promise that "on the third day he will raise us up."

Putting On Our 3D Viewers

This way of reading the Bible in "three dimensions," of listening to how earlier texts shed light on later ones, and how later events repeat and echo earlier ones, is extremely Jewish. We see evidence of it throughout their ancient literature. It's integral to the triennial lectionary, which reads the Torah in light of God's promises for the future.

This style of reading may strike Greek-thinkers as frustratingly inexact and prone to odd, speculative readings. Yes, that is true. But keep in mind that the Scriptures were intimately known, having been read over and over, and connections were being made in retrospect by viewing the narrative as a whole. From a comprehensive knowledge of the text, rabbinic teachers were pointing out patterns and precedents. In effect they were saying, "How does God do things? Well, we see a certain pattern over and over in the Scriptures. Perhaps he'll act this way again."

While rabbinic insights sometimes stretched passages to the limit, they were peculiarly sensitive to repetition and nuances in wording, which the Hebrew Bible's oral composers used quite intentionally to express meaning. Could they have occasionally noticed things we've been missing?

Western Christians overlook many of the connections in the Bible because of our habit of boiling down Scripture into abstract concepts for advanced study. We spend a lot of time discussing the Trinity, even though the term is never used in Scripture. Certainly we find the Father, the Son, and the Spirit throughout the Bible. But instead of following how the *ruach* flows from scene to scene, we prefer to build theological skyscrapers out of abstract definitions instead.

Propositional logic about theological truth can be powerful when it aligns itself with Scripture. Hebraic sensitivity to patterns and repetition can pick up on important themes in the text. Both are useful when they accord with the biblical witness—but lapse into mere speculation when they do not.

A *Figural* Reading of the Bible

The study of the New Testament in light of its interaction with earlier texts (*intertextuality*) is fairly new to Christian scholars and quite of interest in the academic world right now. Just as I was writing this chapter, *Christianity Today* announced its book of the year: *Echoes of Scripture in the Gospels* by Richard Hays, New Testament Professor at Duke Divinity School.[6] Hays has written three books to date that discuss the value of a "figural" reading of the Bible; that is, reading it in terms of how earlier events *prefigure* later ones. This is how he defines it, using a quotation from Erich Auerbach:

> Figural interpretation establishes a connection between two events or persons in such a way that the first signifies not only itself but also the second, while the second involves or fulfills the first. The two poles of a figure are separated in time, but both, being real events or persons, are within temporality. They are both contained in the flowing stream which is historical life, and only the comprehension . . . of the interdependence is a spiritual act.[7]

You may know of an older, related idea of studying the Bible *typologically*, or looking for "types" of Christ in the Old Testament. For instance, Isaac was a "type" of Christ because his father willingly offered him as a sacrifice, and Joseph was a "type" of Christ because he suffered to redeem his family.

What's the difference? Christians in the past have disparaged the Old Testament by regarding it as a hollow shell, as just a collection of "types" and "shadows," devoid of purpose except to predict the coming of Christ, and happily discarded by the Christian church. Western Christians misapply their Greek logic skills, twisting and forcing the text into clear predictions for Jesus to fulfill. We write a shopping list of prophecies and then check each one off in an effort to construct an airtight proof that Jesus is the Christ.

But don't forget that while God made many promises through the prophets, he genuinely loved the nation of Israel and he spoke to their present-day situation. The prophets' main concern was to respond to the matters of their own time. Rather than reading the Hebrew Bible as if it was written *prospectively*, looking only into the future for meaning, a figural reading highlights the idea of reading the New

Testament *retrospectively*, by how it is prefigured by events in the past.

Part of why we do this is to be more sensitive to Jews, for whom the Hebrew Bible *is* the Scriptures. We also don't view the Old Testament as simply written to predict the New Testament, because we see the same phenomenon going on *within* the Old Testament. Noah's ark did not "predict" Moses' ark. The Spirit hovering over the waters of Genesis does not "predict" the Spirit resting on kings and on the Messiah. We see these things *retrospectively*. Similarly, the life of Christ makes much more sense when we view it in light of the scriptural precedents that came before him.

Also, when we don't force the Old Testament into a predictive mode, we find yet more ways that it teaches us about Christ. Jeremiah was indeed rebuking the religious leaders and prophesying the destruction of the temple of his day. The events in his life did not predict the events in Christ's life, yet they did prefigure it. When we look back retrospectively at Christ's prophetic ministry, we see Jeremiah's ministry too. We often see both better when we consider each one in light of the other.

Think of seeing an ultrasound of a developing baby. To an untrained eye, the screen is filled with a confusing collection of blobs and shapes that dance and merge together. Viewed as a whole, these confusing images give us a sneak preview of a child before birth. An experienced technician will be able to imagine what they look like more easily. For parents, little makes sense at the time, but when they look at the same images after the baby is born, sure enough, the infant's distinctive features are obvious. Similarly, we see Christ when we look through the text three-dimensionally and see his image in the Scriptures long before he was born.

TOOLS AND REFLECTIONS

Reading

1. Read the account of the transfiguration in Matthew 17:1–8. Then read the following passages and consider how these scenes prefigure the story in the New Testament.

   Exodus 24:12–18

   Exodus 34:4–10, 28–30

   1 Kings 19:8–14 (Note that Horeb is another name for Sinai)

2. If you lived in the time of Elijah and knew the two passages in Exodus, how would they help you understand why Elijah goes to Horeb in 1 Kings? How did God reveal himself to Elijah compared to Moses?

3. What if we read the transfiguration figurally, viewing it as overlaid on the earlier scenes? God revealed himself on a mountaintop before. What did he reveal about himself this time?

4. Read Malachi 4:4–6. How does this passage recall both Moses and Elijah? What other way was it fulfilled, according to Matthew 17:9–13? (Or see Luke 1:16–17.)

Thoughts for Going Deeper

- Readers will find Richard Hayes, *Echoes of the Scriptures in the Gospels* (Baylor University Press, 2016) and *Reading Backwards* (Baylor University Press, 2014) especially helpful.

12

* * *

Jesus' Bold Messianic Claims

Very Subtle, Very Jewish

Back in the 1980s, there was little in the popular media about the historical Jesus except for the *Jesus Seminar*, with its radical skepticism and its scandalous "discoveries" about Jesus. While the group's sensationalism was roundly criticized, their pessimism about the reliability of the New Testament as a witness to Christ's reality wasn't uncommon in academic circles. I was attending college about this time, and my New Testament professors were also convinced that the Gospels were composed very late and riddled with legends. The words and deeds of the real Jesus were unknowable, they said, and the Christ I worshiped was largely an invention of the Gentile church.

One of their reasons for this theory was that as they read Jesus' words in the more Jewish-sounding Synoptic Gospels (Matthew, Mark, and Luke), they didn't sound much like the exalted claims that John and the rest of the New Testament made about him. As they read Matthew, Mark, and Luke, the Jesus that they found there sounded as if he was just a wandering peasant sage, spinning yarns to teach moral living to the masses. They concluded that Paul, John, and the rest of the New Testament writers were the ones who had exalted him as the Christ. Later, Gentile Christians let their imaginations go wild to concoct fantastic miracle stories they inserted into the Gospels. As *Jesus Seminar* scholar Robert Funk put it,

> The Jesus of the gospels is an imaginative theological construct, into which has been woven traces of that enigmatic sage from Nazareth—traces that cry out for recognition and liberation from the firm grip of those whose faith overpowered their memories.[1]

Many scholars of the time felt the same way, suspecting that Jesus himself never made any claims to be the coming Christ. We could not know Jesus' true, historical reality until we scraped away the "ecclesiastical incrustations" of the later church.

Growing up in a faithful Lutheran home, I had been eager to take college courses to study the Bible at a higher level. But the message that my religion professors communicated was that scholarly inquiry could lead only to disbelief. Discouraged, I put serious Bible study on hold. Instead I poured my energy into getting a PhD in biology, aiming for a career in teaching and research.

Imagine my shock when, years later, I discovered the work of a collaboration of Jewish and Christian scholars who had been studying the Synoptic Gospels together in Jerusalem.[2] As they scrutinized the words of Jesus in their historical setting, they found that he fit perfectly into the world of first-century Judaism, interpreting the Torah and teaching disciples as other early rabbis did. Yet they came to the opposite conclusion as the *Jesus Seminar* scholars about his claims. The closer they looked at Jesus' words, the more they observed his high self-awareness and strong messianic claims. Over and over Jesus said and did things that boldly communicated he was God's promised Messiah.

Why didn't my college professors notice this? Because, like Ed Sanders' audience, they were unaware of the Jewish habit of committing the Scriptures to memory and then referring to them by allusions and subtle references. We don't find Jesus blurting out in so many words, "I'm the Messiah!" Rather, we find him making indirect claims by referring to himself in light of well-known messianic passages from the Scriptures. He was addressing his Jewish audience in a very sophisticated way, drawing continually upon the Scriptures they knew intimately.

Messianic "Hints"

My professors assumed that if Jesus believed he was the Messiah, he would proclaim it from the housetops. But in that religiously charged culture, it would have been gallingly blasphemous to do such a thing. To refer to oneself using a messianic title from the Bible was statement enough. We actually find other self-styled messiahs who took this approach.

Bar Kochba, for instance, had coins minted that referred to himself as *Nasi Yisrael*, "Prince of Israel," suggesting the imagery of Ezekiel 34:24: "My servant David shall be prince among them." Even his self-adopted name, *Bar Kochba*, which literally means "son of the star," reflects the biblical imagery of kings as celestial bodies (Isa. 14:12; 60:1–3) and hints at the messianic prophecy of Numbers 24:17:

> A star shall come out of Jacob,
> and a scepter shall rise out of Israel;
> it shall crush the forehead of Moab
> and break down all the sons of Sheth.

The titles "Prince of Israel" and "Son of the Star" might not sound like much to Christian readers, but if you know the biblical text well, these epithets would ring in your ears as audacious claims to be the fulfillment of ancient prophecy.

Indeed, we see the same phenomenon with Bar Kochba as in the New Testament. Even though Bar Kochba never directly referred to himself as the messiah, Rabbi Akiva and other followers did speak of him this way. Similarly, we find Jesus' disciples were much more expansive about Jesus' identity as "Lord" and "Christ" than Jesus was himself.

Jesus often spoke in the third person using messianic titles, even though it's clear he was talking about himself. For instance, when a paralytic was lowered on a mat into the room where he was teaching, he said, "But that you may know that the Son of Man has authority on earth to forgive sins . . . 'Rise, pick up your bed and go home'" (Matt. 9:6). He's obviously calling himself by the title "Son of Man," but speaking in an oblique way. (More about "Son of Man" later.)

King of Jubilee

If you're unaware of Jesus' Jewish context, his parables and teachings can seem disconnected from the worshipful language that the rest of the New Testament uses to describe him as the Christ. But when you do know his culture, you start hearing him applying powerful prophecies about the coming Messiah to himself.

In Luke 4, we find him preaching from Isaiah 61:1–2.

> The Spirit of the Lord is upon me,
> because he has anointed me
> to proclaim good news to the poor.
> He has sent me to proclaim liberty to the captives
> and recovering of sight to the blind,
> *to set at liberty those who are oppressed,*
> to proclaim the year of the Lord's favor. (Luke 4:18–19, emphasis added)

You should notice immediately that this passage talks about the Lord's "anointing," using a verb related to *mashiach* (anointed one). If you look more closely at this quotation, you'll see Jesus doing some very sophisticated exegesis that is extremely Jewish. Toward the end of the passage he inserted a line from Isaiah 58:6, "to set at liberty those who are oppressed." This was quite intentional, according to New Testament scholar Steven Notley. This is a *gezerah shava* (a comparison of equals), which ties together the passages in Isaiah 58 and Isaiah 61 based on the fact that they share a common phrase, the "Lord's favor."

Both passages relate, poetically, to the announcement of the "year of God's favor," the Year of Jubilee. This was the joyful announcement that all debts are forgiven and families are released from crushing poverty and allowed to return to their ancestral homes. Leviticus 25:10 commands that a Jubilee should be announced every fiftieth year in Israel, but it is unlikely the year of Jubilee was actually observed. Rather, it was seen as something the messianic King would announce when he came.[3]

We know from historical sources that in other nations kings would often proclaim a year of release at the beginning of their reign. They would announce the cancellation of all debts in order to unseat the wealthy and gain favor with the poor. What's fascinating is that when a king announced a year of release, he would also proclaim sins forgiven. In 118 BC, the Egyptian king Ptolemy VIII proclaimed a Jubilee, and the first thing he did was to pardon sins "both intentional and unintentional, except murder and sacrilege."[4]

As we think about the ministry of Jesus, we cannot miss that it was all about proclaiming sins forgiven! Often Jesus tied together the ideas of sin with debt, such as in his parables (like that of the unmerciful servant, Matt. 18:23–35) and in the Lord's Prayer ("forgive us our debts, as we also have forgiven our debtors," Matt. 6:12).

Jesus' brief sermon in Luke 4:18–19 tells us that, as the messianic King, he had proclaimed a year of Jubilee! If you don't know about Jesus' Jewish context, you won't understand that he was claiming to be the Messiah and announcing a kingdom in which sins are forgiven, all in one breath. (Actually, he was doing some other preaching too, which infuriated his listeners, but that is beyond our scope here.[5]) None of these subtle inferences are likely the work of the later Gentile church.

God as "My" Father

Many messianic prophecies describe God's promise that he would one day send a King to rule over Israel who would rule over the whole world. When the Scriptures speak about how a "scepter shall rise out of Israel" (Num. 24:17) or that "the throne of David shall be established before the Lord forever" (1 Kings 2:45), the imagery is that of a valiant king ascending to power.

When twelve-year-old Jesus lingered in the temple to debate with the sages, his parents confronted him after days of frantic searching. Jesus responded by saying, "Didn't you know I had to be in my Father's house?" (Luke 2:49 NIV). Here, his personal reference to God as "*my* Father," *avi*, is quite messianic. The prediction that the Messiah would refer to God as "my Father" is often found in messianic passages (Ps. 89:26; 1 Chron. 17:13) and hearkens back to God's great promise to David in 2 Samuel 7:12–14:

> When your days are fulfilled and you lie down with your fathers, I will raise up your offspring after you, who shall come from your body, and I will establish his kingdom. He shall build a house for my name, and I will establish the throne of his kingdom forever. I will be to him a father, and he shall be to me a son.

One of the most famous of these is Psalm 2, where God's "Son" is announced to the world so that he can be given dominion over it:

> I will surely tell of the decree of the Lord:
> He said to Me, "You are My Son,
> Today I have begotten You.

> Ask of Me, and I will surely give the nations as Your inheritance,
> And the very ends of the earth as Your possession."
> (vv. 7–8 NASB)

Jesus' references to God as "my Father" reflected more than just an intimate affection for God. They would have shocked hearers as a bold statement to be the promised "son of David" who was also the Son of God. Jewish prayer always addresses God as "our Father," in the plural, because Israel as a nation was God's "firstborn son" (Exod. 4:22). Notice that Jesus himself taught his disciples to begin their prayers with "our Father" too. He was unique in addressing God in the singular, as "my" Father.

A Divine Messiah?

When Christians see the phrase "Son of God" they tend to immediately think of divine personhood. It seems obvious to us that this is what this title means. However, his first-century audience may have heard this title as being more about God's chosen king than a divine figure. Why? Because in the ancient world, the imagery of divine sonship was commonly associated with kings.[6] It could denote the fact that a king spoke with the authority of the gods, who expressed their will through him.

Kings of many nations liked to give themselves the title of "son of god." Caesar often stamped this claim on his coins. You could, in fact, read God's promise to David in 2 Samuel 7:14 as saying that a *human* king would come who had such a close relationship with God that he would call him "father."

Because this status was so widely claimed, the title "son of god" may not have sounded like automatic proof of divine identity.[7]

Two other Messianic titles would have actually hinted at a superhuman identity in a much more distinctively Jewish way. One of them, believe it or not, was "Son of Man." For centuries this title perplexed scholars, because the assumption was that it was a way for Christ to speak of himself humbly, as a simple human being, or as a representative human, or the perfect human being. (The phrase "*ben adam*" can indeed be a poetic reference to a human being, as in Ps. 8:4.)

To understand what Jesus was talking about, we need to see how first-century Jews interpreted a messianic prophecy from the book of Daniel about a figure called the "Son of Man."

> As I looked,
> thrones were placed,
> and the Ancient of Days took his seat;
> his clothing was white as snow,
> and the hair of his head like pure wool;
> his throne was fiery flames;
> its wheels were burning fire. . .
> the court sat in judgment,
> and the books were opened. . .
> and behold, with the clouds of heaven
> there came *one like a son of man*,
> and he came to the Ancient of Days
> and was presented before him.
> And to him was given dominion
> and glory and a kingdom,

that all peoples, nations, and languages
  should serve him;
his dominion is an everlasting dominion,
  which shall not pass away,
and his kingdom one
  that shall not be destroyed. (Dan. 7:9–10, 13–14,
    emphasis added)

This passage was universally understood as being about the coming Messiah. The book of Daniel predicted the rise of great kingdoms, which would all eventually fall to the authority of one supreme King who would rule forever. At the pinnacle of his prophecy was this scene of a human-like figure entering God's great throne room, being crowned, and then sitting down on the throne to reign.

Clearly Jesus will fulfill these powerful words when he returns again. Revelation 14:14 says, "I looked, and there before me was a white cloud, and seated on the cloud was one like a son of man with a crown of gold on his head and a sharp sickle in his hand" (NIV).

In Jewish thought, "Son of Man" was one of the most exalted messianic references known.[8] While other passages about the Messiah could be interpreted to say that he'd only be a human king who descended from David's line (2 Sam. 7:12–13 or Ps. 72, for instance), Daniel's vision predicted that the Messiah would somehow be divine. Why? Because of the fact that he comes from heaven, not the earth, and because of the word *like* in the phrase: "one *like* a son of man." This person seemed to be merely a human but was actually far more!

What this vision meant was unclear to its readers. Some thought the "Son of Man" might be an angel, perhaps Michael.

In the years prior to Jesus' ministry, much speculation went on as to what this important prophecy really intended to say.[9]

Simply the fact that this scene in Daniel 7 describes the setting up of a second throne was shocking and controversial. How could there be two thrones in heaven? How could God share his glory with anyone? Much speculation went on in the early centuries AD on this issue that divided Christians and nonbelieving Jews.[10]

The Son of Man as Judge

Several times Jesus spoke about when the Son of Man would come in glory on the clouds, which certainly referred to this passage. One statement Jesus often made was that the Son of Man would be the final judge, as in John 5:27: "And he has given him authority to execute judgment, because he is the Son of Man."

Why? Perhaps you remember from earlier that part of a king's duties was to act as judge (see page 54). He was called to vindicate the innocent, to punish the guilty, and to establish justice in his kingdom. This is the scene we see in the prophecy in Daniel 7 where, just before the Son of Man entered, the books of judgment were opened in preparation for him (see v. 10).

Of course, the king of the world would also be the judge of the whole earth! Think of Jesus' fearsome words in Matthew 25:32 that, as the Son of Man, he would judge all the nations, separating the righteous from the unrighteous. Often we think of Jesus only as our friend and guide, but it's important not to forget that the gentle rabbi of Galilee will also someday be our judge.

Thinking about Jesus' authority to judge is a fearful thing for us. In light of that, the most wonderful use that Jesus made of the title "Son of Man" was when he pointed out his *authority to forgive sin*. A judge has the capacity to condemn, but he also has the power to acquit! Early in Jesus' ministry in Capernaum, when a paralyzed man was lowered into the room by his friends, he said to the paralytic,

> But, so that you may know that the Son of Man has authority on earth to forgive sins . . . I say to you, get up, and pick up your stretcher and go home. (Luke 5:24 NASB)

Even though Jesus had not an ounce of his coming glory, he already had been given the authority of the messianic Judge. But to our great relief, his first exercise of his vast power was to *forgive*.

We also find this incredible message in the story of Zacchaeus, the chief tax collector who repented of his corruption in Luke 19. Zacchaeus had likely swindled his great riches out of the pockets of many impoverished Israelites.[11] But when he repented, Jesus again used his authority as the Son of Man to proclaim salvation to him from his sins. Jesus said,

> Today salvation has come to this house, because this man, too, is a son of Abraham. For the Son of Man came to seek and to save the lost. (vv. 9–10 NIV)

What a great hope we can have that the one who will be our judge wants to forgive our sins even more!

The Divine Shepherd

Most amazingly, this last line from Jesus in the story of Zacchaeus contains not just one powerful hint but two. His words about seeking and saving the lost hearken back to yet another potent messianic image of God's redemption—that of the Divine Shepherd.

When we hear the word *shepherd*, many think of Psalm 23, "The LORD is my shepherd; I shall not want" (v. 1). We love these comforting words. But if you think that this image is only about a soft-focus nursery-school image of Jesus embracing a fuzzy lamb, you'll be greatly surprised by the profound theological implications laden in this title.

A key "shepherd" passage is Isaiah 40. Both Matthew and John connect Isaiah 40:3 with John the Baptist, who was a "voice of one crying in the wilderness" (Matt. 3:3; John 1:23). But then Isaiah 40 goes on to describe the great Shepherd whose arrival he heralds:

> A voice of one calling:
> "In the wilderness prepare
> the way for the LORD;
> make straight in the desert
> a highway for our God." . . .
> You who bring good news to Zion,
> go up on a high mountain.
> You who bring good news to Jerusalem,
> lift up your voice with a shout,
> lift it up, do not be afraid;
> say to the towns of Judah,
> "Here is your God!"
> See, the Sovereign LORD comes with power,
> and he rules with a mighty arm.

> See, his reward is with him,
> and his recompense accompanies him.
> He tends his flock like a shepherd:
> He gathers the lambs in his arms
> and carries them close to his heart;
> he gently leads those that have young.
> (vv. 3, 9–11 NIV)

What is remarkable here is that the Shepherd who arrives is actually the "Sovereign LORD" himself, not a human king or political leader. This passage strongly suggests that the Messiah John the Baptist was proclaiming would be *God incarnate*. Many messianic prophecies describe the coming of a great king but do not imply that he would be divine. But this one implies that God *himself* would be the Shepherd who was to come.[12]

Ezekiel shares another key prophecy about God as the Shepherd of Israel:

> Woe to you shepherds of Israel who only take care of yourselves! Should not shepherds take care of the flock? . . . Because my shepherds did not search for my flock but cared for themselves rather than for my flock . . . I will rescue my flock from their mouths, and it will no longer be food for them.
>
> For this is what the Sovereign LORD says: *I myself* will search for my sheep and look after them. As a shepherd looks after his scattered flock when he is with them, so will I look after my sheep. . . . *I myself* will tend my sheep and have them lie down, declares the Sovereign LORD. *I will search for the lost and bring back the strays.* I will bind up the injured and strengthen the weak, but the sleek and the strong I will destroy. I will shepherd the flock with justice. (Ezek. 34:2, 8, 10–12, 15–16 NIV, emphasis added)[13]

Here, too, the Sovereign LORD is identified as the Shepherd. He himself promises to come to rescue his flock, to search for the lost and bring back the strays. With this in mind, look again at Jesus' words in Luke 19:10:

> *For the Son of Man came to seek and to save the lost.*

Here, the "Son of Man" speaks of Christ's authority to judge and to forgive sins. To "seek and save the lost" alludes to God's promise in Ezekiel, "I will search for the lost and bring back the strays" (34:16 NIV). How much more powerful can you get than that?

In this final line after Jesus' encounter with Zacchaeus, he delivered not just one statement about his mission but two. By hinting to his Scriptures and linking together two key messianic prophecies, he was doing so in a very subtle, sophisticated Jewish way. Jesus wasn't claiming to be the Messiah as just a great human king. He was claiming to be the divine fulfillment of God's most potent promises.

TOOLS AND REFLECTIONS

Reading

1. Read Ezekiel 34:1–31. How do these words sound when you hear echoes of them in the words of Christ? Read John 10:1–6 in light of these ideas.

2. Now read Deuteronomy 30:1–6. Do you hear hints of God's shepherding promise even there? Where does this come in the Torah?

3. Read Matthew 26:63–64, the scene where Jesus was questioned by the high priest. How does knowing that Jesus was alluding to Daniel 7:13–14 and his role as judge expand your understanding of his words?

4. Read Acts 17:22–31, where Paul boils down the gospel to its essence for Gentiles in Athens. How does this fit with what you've learned about Christ's messianic claims?

5. Read Luke 7:36–50. How does your understanding from this chapter deepen your appreciation for this story? How does it speak to your own life?

Thoughts for Going Deeper

- Check out the *Faith Lessons* DVD series by Ray Vander Laan (Zondervan, 1998–2018). These sixteen DVDs study the land and culture of the Bible and highlight Jesus in his Eastern, Jewish context. (Ray Vander Laan was also the teacher at my church who shocked me with news about Jesus' Jewish messianic claims.)

13

When the Words Catch Fire

What We Miss in Isaiah 53

The sun has set and the glow in the sky is fading as we approach the village of Emmaus together. Stumbling in the waning light, I've been oblivious to everything except the burning sensation I've gotten from this whirlwind tour of the Scriptures and Jesus' stunning claims to be the fulfillment of so many messianic promises.

There is a story about a second-century rabbi named Simeon Ben Azzai, a fiery preacher who loved to "string pearls"—to link text after text from the Scriptures. One day he was practically burning the house down! Why? His comment was,

> I was linking up the words of the Torah with one another, and then the words of the Prophets, and the Prophets with the Writings, and the words rejoiced as on the day they were

> delivered from Sinai. And were they not originally delivered from Sinai in fire?[1]

If this was the heart-burning impact of the Scriptures delivered by an ordinary rabbi, you can just start to imagine how much this would be true of Christ!

I hope, in this whirlwind overview, that I've packed some new tools into your cultural toolbox so you can empathize with the communal, family-oriented culture of the biblical world and "be there" as you read. In order to embrace your Pentecost identity as a Bible translator, you'll need to split your thinking to read from the perspective of a first-century disciple but then speak into our world. Hopefully you've gained some new Hebraic thought-categories and discovered the power of reflecting on the Scriptures retrospectively and figurally in order to encounter Christ there.

Now at least you know what "Christ" means, and how different the ancient imagery that surrounded kings was compared to any that we've known. Now you can begin to imagine why the Israelites longed for a king to establish justice on earth in prayers that would resonate with widows in Zambia. Maybe the Scriptures were written for them too.

Yet there is still one question that remains, and it is the one that Jesus himself posed on the Emmaus road:

> Was it not necessary that the Christ should suffer these things and enter into his glory? (Luke 24:26)

We have read all these passages about the promises God made, yet we've barely looked at the one thing that seems to be a monkey wrench in the works: How can one person both suffer and die *and* be a glorious king?

Jesus seemed to think that the answer was self-evident, practically leaping off every page of his Scriptures. I can see how the New Testament says this, but how on earth could Jesus say this was true of the Old Testament?

The answer lies in a key passage—Isaiah 53. It's been well known to many, but with all the tools we've gained for reading, it can unfold as never before. This famous prophecy actually starts in chapter 52. Let's take a tour of Isaiah 52:13–53:12 and see if we don't discover vistas we've never envisioned before.

> Behold, my servant shall act wisely;
> he shall be high and lifted up,
> and shall be exalted.
> As many were astonished at you—
> his appearance was so marred, beyond human semblance,
> and his form beyond that of the children of mankind—
> so shall he sprinkle many nations.
> Kings shall shut their mouths because of him,
> for that which has not been told them they see,
> and that which they have not heard they understand. (52:13–15)

This is the Servant of Isaiah, a mysterious figure who shows his face in four mysterious "Servant Songs." Sometimes his identity merges with that of Israel; sometimes he is clearly separate and acting as the "gatherer of Israel," the one who would bring back God's wandering sheep (see Isa. 42:1–4; 49:1–6; 50:4–9; 52:13–53:12).[2] These visions of redemption overlap and merge, and we can understand each one more deeply when we see it echoing again and again.

The Logic of the Lamb

When we read on in Isaiah 53, we discover that the Servant is not only the messianic Shepherd but also the "lamb who was slain," that concrete metaphor that tears at our emotions, hearkening back to Passover and Abraham's promise to Isaac, "God will provide a lamb."

> All we like sheep have gone astray;
> we have turned—every one—to his own way;
> and the LORD has laid on him
> the iniquity of us all.
> He was oppressed, and he was afflicted,
> yet he opened not his mouth;
> like a lamb that is led to the slaughter,
> and like a sheep that before its shearers is silent,
> so he opened not his mouth.
> By oppression and judgment he was taken away;
> and as for his generation, who considered
> that he was cut off out of the land of the living,
> stricken for the transgression of my people?
> And they made his grave with the wicked
> and with a rich man in his death,
> although he had done no violence,
> and there was no deceit in his mouth.
> (vv. 6–9)

Once again the painful image of the innocent lamb is before us, in all the horrible outrage of laying the sins of the many on one who is innocent. We're left longing for answers. Would a good God do such a thing?

My Greek-ish intellectual side would reach for one of the many volumes on the logic of substitutionary atonement.

But how might a Hebrew answer this question? Rather than constructing a proof, he or she would likely scan the Scriptures, saying that we tiny humans cannot grasp the ways of a Being infinitely beyond us. We understand the character of God by what he's done. So I'd look for a precedent, another situation where God might have let an innocent one suffer because of others. Hmm.

I'd think of Joseph, whose own brothers wanted to kill him and then sold him into slavery. Joseph spent twelve long years in a dank prison in Egypt, convicted of a crime he didn't commit. His own brothers were the ones responsible for putting him there, and they were the ones who deserved to be there! Yet, all in one day, God brought him from the depths of the dungeon to being almost-king of Egypt. Not just so that he could glory in his own success but so that he could prevent his own family from starving in the famine. Not only did Joseph save his family but he saved all of Egypt and the surrounding nations from starving to death too! What humans intended for evil, God intended for good (Gen. 50:20).

I'd conclude that, yes, it is possible for God to allow human evil to serve his own better purposes. He had done it before, so maybe he could do it again.

A Gift Fit for a King

The mournful song of the Servant of Isaiah 53 concludes triumphantly:

> Yet it was the will of the Lord to crush him;
> he has put him to grief;

when his soul makes an offering for guilt,
  he shall see his offspring; he shall prolong his
    days;
the will of the LORD shall prosper in his hand.
Out of the anguish of his soul he shall see and be
    satisfied;
by his knowledge shall the righteous one, my
    servant,
  make many to be accounted righteous,
  and he shall bear their iniquities.
Therefore I will divide him a portion with the many,
  and he shall divide the spoil with the strong,
because he poured out his soul to death
  and was numbered with the transgressors;
yet he bore the sin of many,
  and makes intercession for the transgressors.
    (vv. 10–12)

Finally, we are back in familiar territory here, and I can start to see the gospel presentation I have always known. Christ offered his life to atone for my sins, and because of his sacrifice I can be accounted as righteous before God. Praise the Lord!

Yet there is one line here that seems quite anticlimactic in this joyful, celebratory ode. Look again at Isaiah 53:12:

I will divide him a portion with the many,
  and he shall divide the spoil with the strong.

To our ears this sounds like tepid, halfhearted applause. Along with many others, the Servant will be given a prize, maybe a firm handshake and a pat on the back for all the anguish he endured. Does that seem reasonable?

Our problem is that most English translations obscure the power of this critical line. Listen to how it reads in the New Jewish Publication Society Tanakh (1985 version):

> Assuredly, I will give him the many as his portion,
> He shall receive the multitude as his spoil.

The speaker here is God, and the Servant is not just "among the great." He's being *given the multitudes*. (The verb *halaq*, "to divide, apportion," means to "grant an inheritance" or to "divide" or "apportion" a thing of value, like a conquered territory.) The Servant is not just going to be handed a prize along with other people. The people are actually *his* spoils. He's being *awarded with the people* because of his suffering on their behalf.[3]

Wow. Isn't this a stunning thought? The Suffering Servant doesn't just deserve mild praise, he deserves to have multitudes of people given to him.

You may never have conceived of such a thing—giving a crowd of people to someone as a gift. But we find this same imagery in another significant place in Scripture, the highly messianic Psalm 2:

> The LORD said to me, "You are my Son;
> today I have begotten you.
> Ask of me, and I will make the nations your heritage,
> and the ends of the earth your possession."
> (vv. 7–8)

We've heard Psalm 2 before, where God announces that he has anointed his true King, the Messiah. As God's King is appointed to reign, he is "given" the nations as a gift. The people aren't just his subjects, they are his "possession."

We find similar imagery in Daniel's vision of the Son of Man:

> To him was given dominion
>   and glory and a kingdom,
> that all peoples, nations, and languages
>   should serve him;
> his dominion is an everlasting dominion,
>   which shall not pass away,
> and his kingdom one
>   that shall not be destroyed. (Dan. 7:14)

Here, too, when the Son of Man is exalted, he is awarded with a *kingdom*. All peoples and nations will be his forever and ever.

First the Servant suffers to redeem his people and then he enters his glory by being proclaimed God's true King. It's actually *because* of Christ's suffering that he is given his kingdom! Could this really be true?

The Transformation of Isaiah 53

Reading Isaiah 53:12 in this way transforms the whole emphasis of this Servant's song. Before, this prophecy was only about the Servant's suffering and atonement of sin. But now, Isaiah 53 sounds extremely messianic. Because of his suffering, God's Servant is being granted a kingdom, just like the Son of Man in Daniel 7 and the royal Son of Psalm 2.

Did Jesus read Isaiah 53:12 this way? Well, listen to what Jesus said at the Last Supper. Right after he held up the cup and the bread and announced a new covenant, he said:

> You are those who have stayed with me in my trials, and I assign to you, as my Father assigned to me, a kingdom, that you may eat and drink at my table in my kingdom and sit on thrones judging the twelve tribes of Israel. (Luke 22:28–30)

The language here echoes that of Isaiah 53:12, about Christ being assigned (apportioned, divided) a people and then dividing the spoils with the strong. Just as Jesus will be rewarded for his suffering, so will his disciples who are persecuted on behalf of God's kingdom. They are the "strong" in the sense that they've remained committed to serve God until their last breath, as he has. Note how Paul echoes this idea in Romans 8:16–17: "We are children of God, and if children, then heirs—heirs of God and fellow heirs with Christ, provided we suffer with him in order that we may also be glorified with him."

Just as Jesus will reign over God's kingdom, his disciples will too. Maybe you're uncomfortable with this idea of making kings out of the disciples. Interestingly, the larger context of Luke 22 is Jesus' instruction to his disciples not to seek to be powerful kings but to be humble servants. Immediately beforehand, Jesus said,

> The kings of the Gentiles exercise lordship over them, and those in authority over them are called benefactors. But not so with you. Rather, let the greatest among you become as the youngest, and the leader as one who serves. For who is the greater, one who reclines at table or one who serves? Is it not the one who reclines at table? But I am among you as the one who serves. (Luke 22:25–27)

At the same moment that Jesus speaks of his father granting him a kingdom, he identifies himself as the "one who serves." The connection here seems undeniable. Jesus is claiming to be both the King of Kings and the Servant of Isaiah 53.

I don't know about you, but I'd love to be part of a kingdom where the mightiest leaders are the selfless servants who pour out their energies for the good of the whole. Sounds like a wonderful kind of kingdom to me!

This rereading of Isaiah 53:12 also makes sense out of other New Testament passages that I didn't understand before. The multitudes that Christ is given are the people whose sins he's atoned for. In effect, he's "purchased" them. We find this idea in places like Acts 20:28, where it says that Christ "purchased" the church with his own blood (NASB). Paul put it this way: "You are not your own for you were bought with a price" (1 Cor. 6:19–20). We also hear this in the fact that the apostles often spoke of themselves as *doulos Christou*, "slaves of Christ."

As much as it chafes our modern ears to be called "slaves," it sounds like Jesus' death on the cross did not just pay for our sins—it also purchased our very lives. If we've received Christ as our Savior and Lord, we've actually been *given* to him.

Finding the Gospel in the Gospels

This new understanding of Isaiah 53:12 solved one more important puzzle for me. How does the actual, historical version of *euanggelion* that "Jesus is God's Anointed King" fit together with the gospel I read in evangelism tracts—that if I accept Jesus as my personal Savior, he will pay for all my sins?

Believe it or not, what we've been saying is pretty close, but it's been morphed by Western individualism. We read the Bible as if it was written to each one of us, all by ourselves. We sing praises to Christ for dying for "me personally," and "paying for my sins." Certainly that's true! But the we-focused biblical world spoke of Christ purchasing an *entire kingdom* through his sacrificial death, not just little old me or you.

Listen to the glorious scene in Revelation when the "Lamb" of Isaiah 53 finally takes his throne:

> Then I saw a Lamb, looking as if it had been slain, standing at the center of the throne, encircled by the four living creatures and the elders. . . . And they sang a new song, saying,
>
> "You are worthy to take the scroll
> and to open its seals,
> because you were slain,
> and with your blood you purchased for God
> persons from every tribe and language and people and nation.
> You have made them to be a kingdom and priests to serve our God,
> and they will reign on the earth."
>
> Then I looked and heard the voice of many angels, numbering thousands upon thousands, and ten thousand times ten thousand. . . . In a loud voice they were saying:
>
> "Worthy is the Lamb, who was slain,
> to receive power and wealth and wisdom and strength
> and honor and glory and praise!"
> (Rev. 5:6, 9–12 NIV)

Now Jesus' final proclamation to his disciples that day in Luke 24:46–47 makes sense too: "Thus it is written, that the Christ should suffer and on the third day rise from the dead, and that repentance for the forgiveness of sins should be proclaimed in his name to all nations, beginning from Jerusalem."

The newly crowned messianic King has proclaimed a Jubilee!

TOOLS AND REFLECTIONS

Reading

1. Read Isaiah 52:13 through 53:12 again. Then read Luke 22:14–38, about their final Passover evening. Where do you see Jesus alluding to Isaiah's prophecy?

2. How does having Isaiah's words in mind deepen your understanding of Jesus' words to his disciples? How does verse 12 about being rewarded with the multitudes make a difference?

3. How does the idea of Christ being rewarded with his kingdom come up elsewhere in the New Testament?

4. Read Jeremiah 31:31–34. How do you see this promise being fulfilled in the new covenant that Christ made at the Last Supper?

5. What does a kingdom look like that has its greatest leaders being its humblest servants? What is your role in serving and expanding this kingdom?

Thoughts for Going Deeper

- Check out *Unveiling the Kingdom*, a DVD series by Dwight Pryor about the kingdom of God in Jesus' teaching. This is one of many outstanding resources on his Hebraic context available from the Center for Judaic-Christian Studies at JCStudies.com.
- Consider reading Terence Fretheim, *The Suffering of God* (Minneapolis: Fortress Press, 1984).

Acknowledgments

A book might seem like a solitary task but an entire community is involved. So much professional and scholarly expertise is needed, and many friends and family have blessed the writing of this book.

Many thanks go to Chad Allen and the rest of the team at Baker Publishing. Chad, thanks so much for your enthusiasm for this project and our extra meetings throughout. Jack Kuhatschek, I so appreciate your editorial feedback. Thanks go to Lindsey Spoolstra for her expert oversight of the book editing process and to Patti Brinks for the cover design. To Eileen Hanson and the marketing team: your hard work has helped immensely.

Ann Spangler, thank you for your wise intervention in the publishing world, and for your friendship and willing ear for every question. I appreciate your partnership so much.

Titus Baraka, Milly Erema, Steven Kaziimba, and all my Ugandan friends—I so love learning with you!

Thanks to the many scholars who have taught me so much, including David Bivin, Randall Buth, Steve Notley, Gary and Sharon Alley, and many others. Also, thanks to mentors like Ray Vander Laan and James Whitman who have honed and refined my thinking in so many ways.

Thanks also to the many friends whom I buttonholed into reading the manuscript, including Lisa and Loren Vredevoogd, Keith and Laura Blystra, Lynn Austin, Toby Gruppen, Marcia Johnson, Hillari Madison, Kathleen Van Dyke, Marylin Bright, and Nancy Brown.

Special thanks go to Shirley Hoogeboom for her tenacious grappling with me over these ideas, to Melanie DeKruyter for her creative ideas and wonderful writing help, and to Katherine Setzer for her final edits. And to Andrea Peecher, my minion, for her hard work in my office.

To Elizabeth and Tim West, and Deb and Rick Smith, thank you for your sustaining friendships.

Special thanks go to my precious family, especially David and Lora and the Tverberg girls, as well as my many wise sister-counselors. I've been exceedingly blessed.

Appendix A

Books of the Tanakh

Below are the books of the Scriptures that Jesus read, the Hebrew Bible (Old Testament), as listed in the Jewish Tanakh (TAH-nahk). The word "TaNaKh" is an acronym based on the first letters of the names of its three sections, *Torah* (Law), *Neviim* (Prophets), and *Ketuvim* (Writings).

Torah, "Law" or "Books of Moses"

- Genesis
- Exodus
- Leviticus
- Numbers
- Deuteronomy

Neviim (neh-vee-EEM), or "Prophets"

- Joshua
- Judges
- Samuel 1 & 2
- Kings 1 & 2

- Isaiah
- Jeremiah
- Ezekiel
- Hosea
- Joel
- Amos
- Obadiah
- Jonah
- Micah
- Nahum
- Habakkuk
- Zephaniah
- Haggai
- Zechariah
- Malachi

Ketuvim (keh-too-VEEM), or "Writings"

- Psalms
- Proverbs
- Job
- Song of Solomon
- Ruth
- Lamentations
- Ecclesiastes
- Esther
- Daniel
- Ezra
- Nehemiah
- Chronicles 1 & 2

Appendix B

Thirty Useful Hebrew Words for Bible Study

Hebrew is the "heart language" of the Scriptures that Jesus read, and many words have wider metaphorical meanings that don't carry the same connotations as the corresponding English words. Being aware of language nuances can enrich and deepen Bible study in innumerable ways. Hebrew meanings can be helpful even when reading the New Testament, because often the Greek reflects the Hebraic "accent" of its Jewish authors.

Below is a brief list of some of the most useful, interesting words, along with some of the extended meanings they can have beyond their basic sense. Whenever you encounter one of these words in study, remind yourself of the broader definition and see if it isn't helpful for understanding the passage. This is often useful for understanding differences in translations. (See appendix C for more details on comparing translations.)

Also included is the "Strong's" number, which is a standard numeric identifier for finding original-language words in reference materials. (*Note*: This short guide is *not* meant to be a dictionary, and the descriptions here are not exhaustive, just a helpful start for learners.)

Believe/Faith (*emunah*—H0539) Faith, to us, is confined to our minds, but the biblical word encompasses faithfulness, persistence, and steadfastness, which are the natural outcomes of true faith. When Moses held up his hands all day long until the Israelites won a battle, his arms had *emunah* in the sense of remaining steady (Exod. 17:12).

Bread (*lechem*—H3899) The biblical word for bread is often meant for food more generally, and points to God's provision of our physical needs. In Ruth 1:6, God provided bread for his people by ending the famine. When Jesus taught his disciples to pray for their daily bread, he was talking about their sustenance as a whole (Matt. 6:11).

Evil/Bad (*ra*—H7451) This word basically means "bad," but the sense depends on the context. Often it refers to moral wrong, but it can simply mean harm or misfortune. Psalm 121:7 says that the Lord will "keep you from all [*ra*]," which is often translated "evil" but more likely means "harm."

Fear (*yirah*—H4172) The same Hebrew word can describe emotions that are negative (being afraid or scared), positive (being thrilled or filled with awe), mild (respect), or strong (reverence; Lev. 19:3, 30). *Yirah* can even mean "worship" as it does for the "God-fearers" of the New Testament. The "fear of the Lord" (*yirat Adonai*), biblically, is always understood positively as reverence for God (Prov. 14:26–27).

Forget (*shakach*—H7911) Besides literally forgetting, the word can mean to ignore, or to not act on a request. The cupbearer "forgot" Joseph—meaning he ignored his plea to help him (Gen. 40:23). Likewise, God warned Israel not to "forget" their covenant, in terms of neglecting or forsaking its commands (Deut. 4:23).

Gentiles/Nations (*goyim*—H1471) The same Hebrew word (*goyim*) is used for both "Gentiles" and "nations." This is also true for the Greek word *ethnos* (G1484) in the New Testament. Sometimes *goyim* also has a negative connotation of "idolatrous foreigners." Paul talks about the (*ethne*/*goyim*) being blessed through Abraham (Gal. 3:8) but also rebukes the Corinthians for immorality "not tolerated even among pagans [*ethne*/*goyim*]" (1 Cor. 5:1). Often it's helpful to consider more than one meaning.

Hand/Arm (*yad*—H3027 and *zeroa*—H2220) Both can refer metaphorically to strength or power ("by a mighty hand and an outstretched arm"; Deut. 4:34). One's "right hand" (*yad yamin*) has an even more emphatic sense of strength, and denotes the special favor of a ruler (Exod. 15:6–12).

Hear (*shama*—H8451) Listen, *shema*, but also take heed, understand, be obedient, do what is asked. In fact, almost every place we see the word "obey" in the Bible, it is translated from the verb *shama*, to hear. When Jesus says, "He who has ears, let him hear," he was calling us to put his words into action, not just listen (Matt. 13:9).

Heart (*lev*—H3820 or *levav*—H3824) In Hebrew the "heart" was understood to be not just the seat of the emotions but also the source of all intellect, as well as the seat of the will (Luke 6:45). What are the implications? In Hebraic understanding, using your intellect to study the Bible is an important form of worship!

House (*bayit*—H1004) Often used for one's family, descendants, or possessions (Prov. 14:1), and referring to the temple too. Wordplays often employ its variable meaning in fascinating ways. When King David asked if he could build a "house" for God (a temple), God answered that he would build a "house" for David, meaning a royal lineage that would never end (1 Chron. 17:4, 10). The New Testament proclaims that believers in Christ are God's "house"—his temple, but also his family (Heb. 3:1–6).

Judge/Vindicate (*dan*—H1777 and *shaphat*—H8199) We cringe when we see the word *judgment* (*mishpat*), but this word also means *justice*, and can be quite positive. This is because a judge defends the helpless and vindicates the righteous along with punishing evil. That is why God is praised as a "father to the fatherless, a defender [judge] of widows" (Ps. 68:5 NIV). Also, Rachel named a son "Dan" because God had vindicated her lack of children (Gen. 30:6).

Know (*yadah*—H3045) Rather than being only a mental activity, *yadah* also speaks of relationship and experience, of commitment and loyalty and trust. The word can even denote intimacy, as in Genesis 4:1 when Adam "knew" his wife Eve, and she conceived (KJV). Biblically, a "knowledge of God" (*da'at Elohim*) is not so much about proving God's existence but living in obedient relationship to him (Ps. 91:14; Isa. 11:2).

Law (*torah*—H8451) The "Law" to many Christians is an onerous obligation, a joyless taskmaster. But the Hebrew word actually means "instruction" or "guidance." For instance, the noble wife of Proverbs 31 has a *torah* of *hesed* (teaching of kindness) on her tongue (Prov. 31:26; see also 13:14). Biblically, we should see God as a father lovingly teaching us how to live rather than a heartless lawmaker. This is one of the most misunderstood words in church tradition.

Love (*ahavah*—H0157) Love to us is a warm, sentimental emotion confined to our hearts. To us, it's impossible to love someone you don't even know. The Hebrew word, however, often also refers to the *actions* that result from love—loyalty and doing good for others, so that you can love strangers and even enemies (Lev. 19:34; Luke 6:35).

Messiah (*mashiach*—H4899) Hebrew word for Messiah; Greek is *Christos* (G5547). Literally it means "anointed one," and it refers to the fact that God promised that One would come who would be specially chosen and anointed as a great King (and Priest) for his people (1 Sam. 24:6; Ps. 2:2).

Mercy/Kindness (*hesed*—H2617) Some people wonder where they can find grace in the Old Testament, not realizing that the word *hesed* encompasses this and so much more—a long-suffering love that extends kindness to the undeserving and intervenes on their behalf (Exod. 34:6; Isa. 54:10; Lam. 3:31–32).

Name (*shem*—H8034) The word *shem* often referred to a person's reputation, authority, or identity within a community, rather than to the verbal label that was attached to them (Isa. 56:5). "In the name of Jesus" means "by the authority of Jesus," or "for the sake of Jesus." John 1:12 says, "to all who did receive him, who believed in his name, he gave the right to become children of God." Here, to "believe in his name" means "to believe in Jesus' identity as God's appointed Messiah," or "to submit to his authority as God's King."

Pain/Grief (*atzav*—H6087 and *itzavon*—H6093) When sin in the world became utterly pervasive, God was grieved in his heart (Gen. 6:6). The same pain came upon Adam and Eve, consigning Adam to painful toil in producing food and Eve to painful labor in producing children (Gen. 3:16–17).

Path (*orach*—H0734 and *derek*—H1870) A "path" is the image used to describe the way that we live, and our way of living is called our "walk." Interestingly, the Bible's picture of a road doesn't refer to a paved, multilane highway but to the footprints we follow in and those we leave behind (Ps. 16:11; Isa. 2:3; Heb. 12:13).

Peace (*shalom*—H7965) *Shalom* is not just peacefulness and calm but prosperity and well-being, wholeness and completeness. When a soldier returned from the front, King David asked him about the *shalom* of his commander, the *shalom* of his people, and the *shalom* of the battle (2 Sam. 11:7). When Christ promised his disciples, "[*Shalom*] I leave with you, my [*shalom*] I give to you" (John 14:27), he had much more in mind than just inner calm.

Remember (*zakhar*—H8451) "Do a favor for; come to the aid of." After the flood, God "remembered" Noah and dried up the waters, meaning that he rescued him (Gen. 8:1), and Hannah says God "remembered" her when she conceived—he did her a favor (1 Sam. 1:19). The psalms often plead with God to remember his people in the sense of rescuing them, or "remember [his] mercy" in forgiving sins (Ps. 25:6–7).

Righteous (*tzedek*—H6662) We understand being "righteous" as legal correctness, but the word also encompasses covenantal faithfulness, so that in Jewish Bibles, the "righteous acts of God" is translated as "abundant benevolences" or "gracious deliverances" in terms of how he saved his people in distress (Judg. 5:11; 1 Sam. 12:7; Ps. 35:24). By the first century, "righteousness," *tzedekah*, could also refer to charitable deeds, as in Matthew 6:1–2. Jews still use the word this way today.

Serve (*avad*—H5647) The same word is used for "worship," "work," and "service." And one who does so is an *eved* (H5650), a servant or slave. God redeemed his people from slavery in Egypt so they could serve/worship/work for him, and they were not to be enslaved by anyone else (Lev. 25:42). Paul has this in mind when he calls himself a "servant of Christ" (Rom. 1:1; Phil. 1:1), as does Jesus when he talks about servanthood (Matt. 20:27).

Son (*ben*—H1121) Can mean "descendant," including grandsons and later descendants. The Israelites, both male and female, were called "sons of Israel," and the Messiah was supposed to be a "Son of David" (Matt. 12:23). It was assumed that descendants would take after their forefathers, so a "son of David" would be kingly and powerful. Jesus says peacemakers will be called "sons of God" because they are like God in character (Matt. 5:9).

Soul (*nefesh*—H5315) When Jesus says to "love the Lord with all . . . your soul," the word is *nefesh*, which is not the "soul" as we know it. *Nefesh* is about your life, your breath, and your true self (Gen. 2:7; Deut. 6:5; 10:12).

Shade/Shadow (*tzel*—H6738) In the blazing, withering heat of the desert, nothing is more welcome than the cool of shade. This image is often used for God's protection, as in "The Lord is your keeper; the Lord is your shade on your right hand" (Ps. 91:1; 121:5; Isa. 25:4–5).

Spirit (*ruach*—H7307) We can learn much about God's active, powerful presence in this world and in the lives of believers from the word *ruach*, which means spirit, wind, and breath (Gen. 1:2). When the *ruach* blows through the valley of dry bones to bring new life (Ezek. 37), we see that all of its various meanings are intended. See John 3:8 too.

Vanity/Worthless (*hevel*—H1892) "Vanity of vanities. . . . All is vanity" declares Ecclesiastes 1:2. The word *hevel* means worthless, empty, or fleeting. We don't discuss worthlessness much, but the Bible often does (Jer. 2:5; 16:19; Rom. 3:11).

Visit (*pakad*—H8451) "Pay attention to," in either a positive or negative sense. When God *pakads* a person, he cares for them or comes to their rescue. (Ps. 8:4, "What is man . . . that thou visitests him?" [KJV]). But when he *pakads* an evildoer, he "visits" (punishes) their sins upon them (Jer. 23:2). This fascinating double-edged meaning comes up in several places in both the Old and New Testaments (Luke 19:43–44; 1 Pet. 2:11–12).

Walk (*halakh*—H1980) "Walk" is widely used in Hebrew as a metaphor to describe one's moral lifestyle, as in Psalm 1:1, "Blessed is the man who does not *walk* in the counsel of the wicked" (NASB, emphasis added). In the New Testament also, "walk" (*peripateo*—G4043) is often used this way, like when John tells us to walk as Jesus walked (John 8:12; 1 John 2:6; 2 John 6).

Appendix C

Bible Translations for Word Study

One way to see the range of meanings a biblical word can have is to compare Bible translations. Some translations try to use a very direct, literal English equivalent, even if the words sound a little stilted. Others choose an idiomatic meaning to bring the sense of the passage into modern English. With a bit of comparison of verses and translations, we can often start to get a sense of a word's range of meaning and see why translators made the choices they did. Comparing multiple translations often gives us a better sense of the nuances of the original language than any one translation can on its own.

If you'd like a taste of this kind of study, I've written a short ebook called *5 Hebrew Words That Every Christian Should Know* that is available on Amazon Kindle and at OurRabbiJesus.com. It contains five Hebrew word studies that give readers links to multiple translations so they can be compared.

Here are a few common translations that are useful for study.

Formal Equivalence ("Word for Word")

English Standard Version (ESV)
King James Version (KJV) and New King James Version (NKJV)
New American Standard Bible (NASB)

Balanced Equivalence (Middle of the Road)

Holman Christian Standard Bible (HCSB)
New English Translation (NET)
New International Version (NIV)
New Revised Standard Version (NRSV)

Functional Equivalence ("Thought for Thought")

Contemporary English Translation (CEV)
God's Word (GW)
New Living Translation (NLT)

One highly recommended translation is the *Tanakh: The Holy Scriptures* by the Jewish Publication Society (1985 version, or NJPS), which is very sophisticated in catching poetic phrasing and idiomatic language. This is not the 1917 version, which is in the public domain. The NJPS is an utterly new rendering of the Hebrew texts, and is not at all like the "old" JPS.

Another interesting resource is Everett Fox's *The Five Books of Moses* (New York: Shocken, 1995). It renders the Hebrew hyperliterally to allow readers to hear the poetry and repetition of the original wording.

What I haven't found terribly useful are Bibles that change proper names to Hebrew-sounding equivalents (Jesus to Yeshua, Paul to Sha'ul, James to Ya'akov, etc.). While the names are pronounced more realistically, this doesn't help with understanding language nuances. Paraphrases such as *The Message* are also not useful for word study because they render the original language so loosely.

Notes

Chapter 1 Opening the Bible with Jesus

1. See, for instance, Craig Evans, *Fabricating Jesus: How Modern Scholars Distort the Gospels* (Downers Grove, IL: InterVarsity Press, 2006), 100–122. Urban areas felt the Greeks' influence and some aristocrats embraced Hellenism, but the Galilean villages where Jesus preached were highly observant and religiously conservative. For more about the religious setting of pre-70 AD Galilee, see Shmuel Safrai, "The Jewish Cultural Nature of the Galilee in the First Century," *Immanuel* 24/25 (1990): 147–86.

2. Anson Rainey and Steven Notley, *The Sacred Bridge: Carta's Atlas of the Biblical World* (Carta: Jerusalem, 2006), 367–68. Also see Carsten Peter Thiede, *The Emmaus Mystery* (New York: Continuum, 2005).

3. Throughout this book I often use "Old Testament" rather than "Hebrew Bible" or "Tanakh" because it is familiar to general Christian audiences, even though the term conveys an unfortunate sense of obsoleteness. Since many readers are new to contextual issues, I find it better to use familiar terms rather than asking readers to continually digest new vocabulary. Often I just use "Scriptures."

4. Kenneth Bailey, *The Cross and the Prodigal* (St. Louis: Concordia, 1973), 9.

5. Kenneth Bailey, *Finding the Lost Cultural Keys to Luke 15* (St. Louis: Concordia, 1992), Kindle loc. 403–6.

Chapter 2 Learning to Be There

1. Simcha Raz and Edward Levin, *The Sayings of Rabbi Menachem Mendel of Kotz* (New York: Roman & Littlefield, 1995), 149. Rabbi Mendel lived between 1787 and 1859.

2. For more on that subject, see Andrew Sullivan, "I Used to Be a Human Being," *New York Magazine*, September 2016, http://nymag.com/selectall/2016/09/andrew-sullivan-technology-almost-killed-me.html.

3. Malcolm Gladwell, "The Ethnic Theory of Plane Crashes," in *Outliers* (New York: Little, Brown & Co, 2008), 177–223.

4. Robert Funk, *Honest to Jesus: Jesus for a New Millennium* (San Francisco: Harper Collins, 1997), 314.

5. Sandra Richter, *The Epic of Eden* (Downers Grove, IL: InterVarsity Press, 2008), 38.

6. Eugene Nida, *Meaning Across Cultures* (Maryknoll, NY: Orbis, 1981), 29.

7. See Jackson Wu, *One Gospel for All Nations: A Practical Approach to Biblical Contextualization* (Pasadena, CA: William Carey Library, 2015). In his book he defends the idea that the gospel needs to be contextualized for the Chinese and then he spells out how it would sound in their communal, honor-shame oriented culture. From my knowledge of the collectivist nature of ancient Judaism, the assumptions that he described in Chinese culture sounded quite similar to those of the biblical world.

8. Joseph Henrich, Steven Heine, and Ara Norenzayan, "The Weirdest People in the World," *Behavioral and Brain Sciences* 33 (2010): 61–135.

9. Phillip Jenkins, "The Power of the Bible in the Global South," *The Christian Century* (July 11, 2006), 22–26.

Chapter 3 What Does "Christ" Mean, Anyway?

1. For more on the idea of the Messiah within the concept of kingship in Israel, see Roland deVaux, *Ancient Israel: Its Life and Institutions* (London: Dartmon, Longman and Todd, 1994), 100–114; and Sigmund Mowinckel, *He That Cometh* (Grand Rapids: Eerdmans, 2005).

2. Gary Haugen, "The Hidden Reason for Poverty the World Needs to Address Now," TED2015, 22:08, filmed March 2015, https://www.ted.com/talks/gary_haugen_the_hidden_reason_for_poverty_the_world_needs_to_address_now.

3. Ibid.

4. From the Wisdom of Solomon 6:1–7, an extracanonical book written between 100–200 BC. Similar statements are made in Luke 12:48 and James 3:1.

Chapter 4 Painting in Hebrew

1. This figure is the size of biblical Hebrew, which only includes words recorded in the Bible. The actual number would have been slightly larger but still a small fraction of many modern languages. The size is not that different than other oral indigenous languages, which tend to be small because words fall out of use if not recorded in print.

English is actually unusually large because of its history of absorbing terms from other languages. For comparison, it has about twice as many commonly used words as French. This gives it an unusual ability to express fine shades of meaning. See Bill Bryson, *The Mother Tongue: English and How It Got That Way* (New York: Harper Collins, 1990), 13.

2. Jules Michelet, *The Life of Luther from His Own Writings* (London: Whittaker, 1846), 283.

3. See Dave Brunn, *One Bible, Many Versions* (Downers Grove, IL: InterVarsity Press, 2013). From his experience as a Bible translator in Papua New Guinea, Brunn discusses the difficulty of Bible translation between completely unrelated languages.

4. The fact that Hebrew word meanings are so helpful to Bible readers is not because the language is magical but because it comes from a very different cultural and linguistic background and includes many words for concepts that go unnamed in Greek or English. Christians are largely unaware of this because they always read the Bible in translation. In order to highlight the contrast between our language and that of the Bible that Jesus read and preached, this book focuses on nuances of Hebrew words, leaving readers to learn Greek vocabulary elsewhere.

5. See Gunther Ebel, "Peripateo," in *The New International Dictionary of New Testament Theology*, vol. 3, ed. Colin Brown (Grand Rapids: Zondervan, 1978), 943–45. Some have thought that Semitic Greek in the New Testament reflects Aramaic, or that the authors were imitating the style of the Septuagint, the Greek translation of the Old Testament. The Septuagint doesn't actually translate *halakh* as *peripateo* in Greek.

Several other Hebraisms in the New Testament reflect the usage of Hebrew as it was spoken in the first century (Mishnaic Hebrew), not in the time of the Old Testament. Aramaic was a closely related language to Hebrew, and Jesus was fluent in both. When Jesus preached from the Scriptures or told parables, he was almost certainly speaking Hebrew. Rabbinic parables were always in Hebrew, even centuries later, after Aramaic became dominant. Also, Jesus' *gezerah shava* connections between Scripture passages were in Hebrew, not Aramaic. The connection that he made in Luke 4 between Isaiah 61 and 58 only works in Hebrew (see page 228). For more, see R. Steven Notley and Randall Buth, eds., *The Language Environment of First Century Judaea* (Leiden: Brill, 2014). Also see Dr. Notley, "Between the Chairs: New Testament Evidence of the Hebrew that Jesus Spoke," lecture, Lanier Theological Library, accessed June 30, 2016, https://www.youtube.com/watch?v=cuPDW_3RtJQ.

6. Michelet, *The Life of Luther from His Own Writings*, 284.

7. In this phrase *yirah* is in the construct form, *yirat* (yeer-AHT), meaning that it is "attached" to the next word. Words that end in the letter *heh* (an "h" sound) adopt a *tav* (a "t" sound) instead. Another example is *Simchat Torah* (sim-HAHT tor-AH), "the Joy of the Torah," the celebration when the weekly Torah reading begins again in Genesis. Normally the word for joy is *simchah* (sim-HAH) but here it is in the construct form, connected to the word *torah*.

8. Abraham Joshua Heschel, *God in Search of Man* (New York: Farrar, Straus and Giroux, 1955), 76–77.

9. For more on the idiom of the "bad eye" and its opposite, the "good eye," as referring to stinginess and generosity, see the chapter "Gaining a Good Eye" in Lois Tverberg, *Walking in the Dust of Rabbi Jesus* (Grand Rapids: Zondervan, 2012), 69–79.

Chapter 5 Greek Brain, Hebrew Brain

1. Roger Newton, *Galileo's Pendulum: From the Rhythm of Time to the Making of Matter* (Cambridge: Harvard University Press, 2009), 1.

2. This is a classic statement from Descartes, a seventeenth-century French philosopher. I include it because it illustrates the logic of rationalism.

3. Bradley W. Patterson, *Redefining Reason* (Xlibris, 2011), Google ebook, 177.

4. Walter Ong points out that the rise of literacy in the ancient world may have contributed to Western thought too. Oral, nonliterate cultures tend to communicate in concrete images rather than in abstractions as modern Westerners do. Ong theorizes that when a culture is widely literate, people start communicating in more complex abstractions because longer chains of reasoning can be recorded in print. Also, ideas become more objective and detached from personal experience when the source is a book rather than a person. See Walter Ong, *Orality and Literacy* (New York: Routledge, 1982).

5. Gary Burge, *Jesus, the Middle Eastern Storyteller* (Grand Rapids: Zondervan, 2009), 21–22.

6. Ken Bailey, *Finding the Lost: Cultural Keys to Luke 15* (St. Louis, MO: Concordia, 1992), 21.

7. Ibid.

8. George Orwell, "Politics and the English Language" in *George Orwell: In Front of Your Nose, 1946–1950* (Boston: Godine, 2000), 133.

9. See Eric Havelock, "The Alphabetic Mind: A Gift of Greece to the Modern World," *Oral Tradition* 1, no. 1 (1986): 134–50.

10. Brunn, *One Bible, Many Versions*, 142–45.

11. The two words in Hebrew that are translated as "love" are *ahava* and *hesed*. The word *ahava* describes love between friends and family members. The word *hesed* is more about long-term covenantal love that can be expressed as mercy or kindness.

12. Nahum Sarna, *The JPS Torah Commentary: Genesis* (New York: Jewish Publication Society, 1989), 17.

13. For more on the complex, artful use of concrete imagery in OT narrative, see Robert Altar, *The Art of Biblical Narrative* (New York: Basic Books, 1981).

14. For more, see *Sitting at the Feet of Rabbi Jesus*, 180–96. When John asked Jesus (via a disciple) if he was the one to come, Jesus responded by quoting multiple prophecies about healing and mercy in the messianic age (Matt. 11:2–4). See also *Walking in the Dust of Rabbi Jesus*, 146–48.

15. For more about Jesus' parables within their Jewish setting, see Brad Young, *Jesus the Jewish Theologian* (Peabody, MA: Hendrickson, 1995). For more analysis, see R. Steven Notley and Ze'ev Safrai, *The Parables of the Sages* (Jerusalem: Carta, 2011); and Brad Young, *The Parables* (Peabody, MA: Hendrickson, 1998).

16. Galileo Galilei, Andrea Frova, and Mariapiera Marenzana, *Thus Spoke Galileo: The Great Scientist's Ideas and Their Relevance to the Present Day* (New York: Oxford University Press, 2006), 121–23.

17. John MacArthur, "Understanding the Sabbath," sermon, *Grace to You*, September 20, 2009. (See *Walking in the Dust of Rabbi Jesus*, 23.)

18. The implications are, of course, that Jewish believers in Jesus are still called to live according to the Torah. Not to "earn" salvation but because God's ongoing covenant with Israel gave this nation distinctive laws to set it apart from all others. For more, see David Rudolf and Joel Willitts, eds., *Introduction to Messianic Judaism* (Grand Rapids: Zondervan, 2013); or Mark Kinzer, *Post-Missionary Messianic Judaism* (Grand Rapids: Brazos Press, 2005).

19. Karl Barth, *Dogmatics in Outline* (New York: Harper, 1959), 31.

20. See chapter 2 in my book *Walking in the Dust of Rabbi Jesus*, 31–41, for a lengthy discussion on the *Shema*.

21. For more on what table fellowship meant in the time of Christ, see *Sitting at the Feet of Rabbi Jesus*, 128–44.

Chapter 6 Why Jesus Needs Those Boring "Begats"

1. Ryszard Kapuscinski, *The Shadow of the Sun* (New York: Random House, 2002), 205.

2. And of course, homosexual activity was prohibited in both the OT and NT. We assume that marriage legalizes sexual activity, but it did not do that for prohibited unions such as that between a man and his sister, his aunt, or other relatives. They simply could not get married.

3. For more, see Ken Campbell, *Marriage and Family in the Biblical World* (Downers Grove, IL: IVP Academic, 2003).

4. A. Chadwick Thornhill, *The Chosen People: Election, Paul and Second Temple Judaism* (Downers Grove, IL: InterVarsity Press, 2015), 135–46.

Chapter 7 Reading the Bible as a "We"

1. *Your* Personalized Bible, based on the World English Bible (public domain) (Richland, VA: Phronesis, 2013). The italicized "Your" is actually part of the title, in order to emphasize how much this Bible is for *you*, personally.

2. There is one place in Paul's writing where he talks about a believer's body as being a temple for the Spirit (1 Cor. 6:19). But overwhelmingly, whenever he talks about temples, he's speaking communally. See Gerald Hawthorne and Ralph Martin, *The Dictionary of Paul and His Letters* (Downers Grove, IL: InterVarsity Press, 1993), 127.

3. Kapuscinski, *Shadow of the Sun*, 36.

4. Sarah Lanier, *Foreign to Familiar: A Guide to Understanding Hot- and Cold-Climate Cultures* (Hagerstown, MD: McDougal Publishing, 2000), 45.

5. Women who take their husband's name, obviously, give up their own family's reputation. But since traditionally they invested themselves in building a new family, that was the name they'd take. My ancestors in Norway would leave the entire farm to the eldest son, leaving the younger sons with nothing, because the eldest was responsible for supporting his parents in their old age. Daughters of a poor family actually had more chance for social mobility than younger sons, because they could marry "upward."

6. Many people overly focus on the spelling and pronunciation of names because they narrowly focus on the "verbal identifying label" aspect of "name,"

rather than grasping that the word *shem* also refers to one's identity, reputation, or renown.

7. Jacob Milgrom, *The JPS Torah Commentary: Numbers* (New York: Jewish Publication Society), 127, 410–13.

8. Michael Fishbane, *The JPS Bible Commentary: Haftarot* (New York, Jewish Publication Society, 2002), 296. In Hebrew, single and plural forms can both be used in the same verse. Sometimes the singular second person address is even feminine, when Zion or Jerusalem is used for a personification as the people of Israel.

9. C. S. Lewis, *The Chronicles of Narnia: The Lion, the Witch and the Wardrobe* (New York: MacMillan, 1950), 178–79.

10. Nahum Sarna, *Understanding Genesis* (New York: Shocken Books, 1966), 150–51.

11. Solomon Schechter, *Aspects of Rabbinic Theology* (Grand Rapids: Baker, 1998), 170–98.

12. For a fascinating commentary on the *Akedah* and its interpretation in Jewish thought, see Shalom Spiegel, *The Last Trial* (New York: Berman House, 1979).

Chapter 8 Like Grasshoppers in Our Own Eyes

1. James Kugel, *The Great Poems of the Bible* (New York: Simon and Schuster, 1999), 30–43.

2. Ibid.

3. Abraham Joshua Heschel, *God in Search of Man* (New York: Ferrar, Straus and Giroux, 1955), 36.

4. See John Levenson's excellent chapter, "Why Jews Are Not Interested in Biblical Theology" in *The Hebrew Bible, the Old Testament, and Historical Criticism* (Louisville: Westminster John Knox, 1993), 31–61.

5. Kugel, *Great Poems of the Bible*, 30–43.

6. Ibid.

7. See Ziony Zevit, "Three Ways to Look at the Ten Plagues," *Bible Review* 6, no. 3 (June 1990): 16–23, 42. Note that Numbers 33:4 declares that "the LORD had brought judgment on their gods" (NIV).

8. For more on prayers of blessing, see Ann Spangler and Lois Tverberg, *Sitting at the Feet of Rabbi Jesus* (Grand Rapids: Zondervan, 2009), especially the chapter "For Everything a Blessing" and the appendix list of blessings.

9. Sarna, *Understanding Genesis*, 4–18.

10. Moshe Greenberg, "Some Postulates of Biblical Law" in *Essential Papers on Israel and the Ancient Near East*, ed. Fredrick Greenspahn (New York: NYU Press, 1991), 333–52.

11. Greenberg comments that by the New Testament era, the Jewish law code had absorbed the idea that human life is precious to the point where it made capital punishment exceedingly rare. Even the life of the murderer is still precious to God.

Chapter 9 Memory Is Critical

1. See E. P. Sanders, "Paul's Jewishness," in *Paul's Jewish Matrix*, ed. T. G. Casey and J. Taylor (Rome: Gregorian & Biblical Press, 2001), 50–63.

2. Martin Jaffee, "Ontologies of Textuality in Classical Rabbinic Judaism," in *Voice, Text, Hypertext*, ed. Raimonda Modiano, Leroy Searle, and Peter L. Shillingsburg (Seattle: University of Washington Press, 2004), 89.

3. Eric Havelock, *Preface to Plato* (Cambridge: Harvard University Press, 2009), 27.

4. Shmuel Safrai and Menahem Stern, eds., *The Jewish People in the First Century* (Amsterdam: Van Gorcum, 1976), 953.

5. Babylonian Talmud, Hagiga 9[b].

6. Safrai and Stern, *Jewish People in the First Century*, 968.

7. This quotation is attributed to Rabbi Simeon ben Yohai, who lived between 100–160 AD. For more, see Jordan Rosenblum, *Food and Identity in Early Judaism* (Cambridge: Cambridge University Press, 2010), 132.

8. According to the Jerusalem Talmud, Megilla 2:5, Rabbi Meir, who lived in the Galilee in the second century, visited a village that didn't have a scroll of Esther, so he wrote one for them himself.

9. C. S. Lewis, *The Literary Impact of the Authorized Version* (Philadelphia: Fortress Press, 1963), 28.

10. When I first heard about this I simply didn't believe it. Now, after twenty years of reading Jewish writing, I've seen it often. For instance, Abraham Heschel's *God in Search of Man* is filled with references to both the Bible and rabbinic literature. A few are cited and many more are simply interwoven into the text. Often Christians are told to read *God in Search of Man* as an introduction to Jewish thought, but find it slow going because so much is laid between the lines. Heschel has commented that not one word he writes does not originate from the Bible or from rabbinic thought. For more on this topic, see chapter 3, "Stringing Pearls," in *Sitting at the Feet of Rabbi Jesus*, 36–49.

11. R. Steven Notley and Jeff Garcia, "Hebrew-Only Exegesis: A Philological Approach to Jesus' Use of the Hebrew Bible," in *The Language Environment of First Century Judaea*, vol. 2 (Leiden: Brill, 2014), 370–71.

12. You can read these sermons in a collection of Jewish literature called *Midrash*. In later centuries, rabbis grew ever more creative in inventing ways to draw a sermon lesson out of a text. In the centuries after the New Testament period, rabbinic teachers began to derive meanings from how Hebrew words were spelled or by adding up the numerical equivalent of the letters. These overly creative techniques were not yet in use in the first century. See David Instone Brewer, *Techniques and Assumptions in Jewish Exegesis before 70 AD* (Tubigen: Mohr Siebeck, 1992).

13. Richter, *Epic of Eden*, 17.

Chapter 10 Moses and the Prophets Have Spoken

1. Slight differences exist in the readings between Jewish congregations from different regions. The two largest groups are the European (Ashkenazi) and Sephardic (Spanish and North African) Jews. A few communities have even preserved some of the triennial prophetic readings, even though they read through the Torah annually.

2. Pirke Avot 5:22, from Ben Bag Bag, a disciple of Hillel who lived in the early first century.

3. For a discussion of the differences between the annual and triennial *haftarot*, see Michael Fishbane, *JPS Bible Commentary: Haftarot* (New York: Jewish Publication Society), xix–xxxii. For the triennial readings referenced in this chapter, see Charles Perrot, "The Reading of the Bible in the Ancient Synagogue," in *Mikra*, ed. Martin Mulder (Philadelphia: Fortress Press, 1988), 137–59.

In the past century, many modern congregations have switched to a three-year schedule that is based on the annual Torah calendar. They read from Genesis through Deuteronomy each year, but read only a third of a lesson each week, alternating by year. The ancient triennial schedule did not try to align with the yearly calendar. It likely took about three and a half years. In the older triennial tradition, the Torah portion was not called a *parashah* but a *seder* (pl. *sederim*). The prophetic readings in both the annual and triennial traditions are called *haftarot*.

4. Isaiah is much less common in the annual lectionary, with the exception of the last few weeks of the year, when Deuteronomy is read. The reason Isaiah is prominent then isn't actually because it relates to the Torah but rather because in the final weeks before the Holy Days passages of consolation from Isaiah are traditionally read.

5. See Luke 7:27, where Jesus quotes a combination of Exodus 23:20 and Malachi 3:1 in reference to John the Baptist. ("Behold, I send my messenger before your face, who will prepare your way before you.") Malachi 3 is the triennial *haftarah* reading for Exodus 23:20. (See Mark 1:2 too.)

6. See Steven Di Mattei, "Paul's Allegory of the Two Covenants (Gal. 4.21–31) in Light of First-Century Hellenistic Rhetoric and Jewish Hermeneutics," in *New Testament Studies* 52 (November 2006): 102–22. Another "magnetized" lesson found in the triennial lectionary appears in 2 Corinthians 3:6–18, which is based on Exodus 34:27–35 and Jeremiah 31:32–39. One scholar reports that Philo, a first-century Jewish philosopher in Egypt, was aware of a triennial lectionary too. See Naomi Cohen, *Philo's Scriptures: Citations from the Prophets and Writings: Evidence for a Haftarah Cycle in Second Temple Judaism* (Leiden, Netherlands: Brill, 2007).

7. See Safrai and Stern, "Jewish Cultural Nature of the Galilee in the First Century."

8. Hymns (*piyyut*) that were based on the triennial readings were also composed in Hebrew. Regarding Aramaic, *targums* did not come into use until after 70 AD, according to scholar Daniel Machiela. See, "Hebrew, Aramaic, and the Differing Phenomena of Targum and Translation in the Second Temple Period and Post-Second Temple Period," in *The Language Environment of First Century Judaea* (Leiden: Brill, 2014), 209–45.

9. Hananel Mack, "What Happened to Jesus' Haftarah?" *HaAretz* (August 12, 2005), http://www.haaretz.com/news/what-happened-to-jesus-haftarah-1.166699. Other scholars have noted this too.

10. A personal observation. The Geniza lectionaries appear to date from about the ninth century. They record the earlier triennial tradition that continued to be used in synagogues in Cairo until about 1100 AD.

Chapter 11 Reading in the Third Dimension

1. An excellent set of commentaries that is very sensitive to connections is the *JPS Torah Commentary* series (New York: Jewish Publication Society). Also, Umberto Cassuto's commentaries on Genesis and Exodus are classics.

2. See John Walton's *The Lost World of Genesis One* (Downers Grove, IL: IVP Academic, 2009) for more about how the creation account would have been understood in Abraham's day. He also points out that we need to "be there" culturally rather than expect the Bible to address modern scientific questions.

3. Genesis Rabbah 2:4. Genesis Rabbah is a collection of rabbinic sermons on Genesis that dates from between 300–500 AD and records insights from earlier centuries. *Rabbah* means "great" in the sense of being an expansive commentary on the text.

4. Genesis Rabbah 56.

5. Pinchas Lapide, *The Resurrection of Jesus: A Jewish Perspective* (Minneapolis: Augsburg Fortress, 1982), 91–93.

6. See Richard Hayes, *Echoes of Scripture in the Letters of Paul* (New Haven: Yale University Press, 1989); *Reading Backwards* (Waco: Baylor University Press, 2014); and *Echoes of Scripture in the Gospels* (Waco: Baylor University Press, 2016) for more.

7. Erich Auerbach, *Mimesis* (Princeton: Princeton University Press, 1968), 73.

Chapter 12 Jesus' Bold Messianic Claims

1. Robert Funk, *The Five Gospels: What Did Jesus Really Say? The Search for the Authentic Words of Jesus* (New York: Macmillan, 1996), 4.

2. I'm speaking of the *Jerusalem School of Synoptic Research*, which is a think tank of Jewish and Christian scholars who aim to bring historical, linguistic, and critical expertise to bear on the Synoptic Gospels in order to resituate Jesus in his first-century Jewish context.

3. The idea that the Messiah would announce a Jubilee by proclaiming Isaiah 61 had been fulfilled was found in the Dead Sea Scrolls, 11Q13.

4. See Moshe Weinfeld, "Sabbatical Year and Jubilee in the Pentateuchal Laws and Their Ancient Near Eastern Background," in *Law in the Bible and Its Environment* (Gottingen: Vandenhoeck and Ruprecht, 1990), 173. Intriguingly, in Leviticus 25:9 God decreed that the Jubilee year be announced on the Day of Atonement, when he forgave all the sins of Israel.

5. See R. Steven Notley, "First-Century Jewish Use of Scripture: Evidence from the Life of Jesus," *Jerusalem Perspective*, January 1, 2004, http://www.jerusalemperspective.com/4309/.

6. Sometimes this title was used in other ways too. Greeks spoke of legendary heroes as "sons of God." In the Hebrew Bible, the phrase *benei Elohim* could refer to angels, as in Job 1:6.

7. See James Dunn, *Jesus Remembered* (Grand Rapids: Eerdmans, 2003), 709–10.

8. David Flusser with R. Steven Notley, *The Sage from Galilee* (Grand Rapids: Eerdmans, 2007), 107–16. Also Brad Young, *Jesus the Jewish Theologian* (Peabody, MA: Hendrikson, 1995), 243–52.

9. See 1 Enoch 46. The book of 1 Enoch is a noncanonical Jewish text from about two hundred years before Jesus. While not authoritative, it can show us Jewish thinking from around the period when Jesus lived.

10. See Alan Segal, *Two Powers in Heaven: Early Rabbinic Reports of Christianity and Gnosticism* (Leiden, Netherlands: Brill, 2002).

11. I disagree with commentaries that portray Zacchaeus as a good-hearted man who was unfairly excluded because he was in the wrong profession. In a communal society, it would have been outrageous to betray one's family by siding with Roman overlords to profit at his people's expense.

12. See David Flusser, *The Sage from Galilee: Rediscovering Jesus' Jewishness* (Grand Rapids: Eerdmans, 2007), 31–32.

13. There are similar prophecies in Jeremiah 23:1–5 and Zechariah 10:3.

Chapter 13 When the Words Catch Fire

1. Leviticus Rabbah 16:4.

2. You may have read interpreters who say that "the Servant" always refers to the nation of Israel in Isaiah. This is not true. Earlier, on page 148, I pointed out how the Bible often poetically identifies a leader with that of the group he leads, because of its collective thinking. The Servant Songs of Isaiah are just one of many places where the text shifts back and forth between speaking of an individual and of a group.

3. See J. W. Olley, "'The Many:' How is Isaiah 53:12a to Be Understood?" *Biblica* 68 (1987): 330–56; and Jan L. Koole, *Isaiah III, Volume 2: Isaiah 49–55* (Belgium: Peeters, 1998), 336–39. More than four pages are spent in Leuven's volume to analyze this one line, explaining that while the translation we find above (ESV) is admissible, it's actually less likely to reflect the meaning than the one in the NJPS Tanakh.

The Septuagint, the Greek translation of the Old Testament from the third century BC, reflects the same interpretation of Isaiah 53:12 as the NJPS Tanakh: "Because of this, he will inherit the multitudes and to the mighty he will distribute the plunder." The NJPS interprets the second half of verse 12 as a parallelism with the first half, but it can be read either way, as either that God will apportion the spoils to the Servant, or that the Servant will apportion the spoils to the strong. It looks from Luke 22:29 that Jesus interpreted it the second way.

Recommended Resources

Bailey, Kenneth E. *Jesus through Middle Eastern Eyes*. Downers Grove, IL: IVP Academic, 2008.

———. *Poet and Peasant and Through Peasant Eyes*, combined ed. Grand Rapids: Eerdmans, 1983.

Bivin, David. *New Light on the Difficult Words of Jesus: Insights from His Jewish Context*. Holland, MI: En-Gedi Resource Center, 2005.

Boyarin, Daniel. The Jewish Gospels: The Story of the Jewish Gospels. New York: The New Press, 2012.

Brunn, Dave. *One Bible, Many Versions: Are All Translations Created Equal?* Downers Grove, IL: InterVarsity Press, 2013.

Burge, Gary. *Jesus, the Middle Eastern Storyteller*. Grand Rapids: Zondervan, 2009.

Dickson, Athol. *The Gospel According to Moses: What My Jewish Friends Taught Me about Jesus*. Grand Rapids: Brazos Press, 2003.

Flusser, David with R. Steven Notley. *The Sage from Galilee: Rediscovering Jesus' Genius*. Grand Rapids: Eerdmans, 2007.

Haidt, Jonathan. *The Righteous Mind*. New York: Pantheon, 2012.

Hammer, Reuven. *The Torah Revolution: Fourteen Truths That Changed the World*. Woodstock, VT: Jewish Lights Publishing, 2011.

Hayes, Richard. *Echoes of Scripture in the Gospels*. Waco: Baylor University Press, 2016.

———. *Echoes of Scripture in the Letters of Paul*. New Haven: Yale University Press, 1989.

———. *Reading Backwards*. Waco: Baylor University Press, 2014.

Heschel, Abraham. *God in Search of Man: A Philosophy of Judaism*. New York: Farrar Straus Giroux, 1976.

———. *The Prophets*. New York: Harper and Row, 1962.

Kaiser, Walter and Duane Garrett. *Archaeological Study Bible: An Illustrated Walk through Biblical History and Culture*. Grand Rapids: Zondervan, 2006.

Knohl, Israel. The Messiah before Jesus: The Suffering Servant of the Dead Sea Scrolls. Berkeley: University of California Press, 2000.

Lanier, Sarah. *Foreign to Familiar: A Guide to Understanding Hot- and Cold-Climate Cultures*. Hagerstown, MD: McDougal Publishing, 2000.

Lapide, Pinchas. *The Resurrection of Jesus: A Jewish Perspective*. Eugene, OR: Wipf & Stock, 1982.

Nida, Eugene. *Meaning Across Cultures*. Maryknoll, NY: Orbis, 1981.

Pearl, Chaim. *Theology in Rabbinic Stories*. Peabody, MA: Hendrickson, 1997.

Provan, Iain. *Seriously Dangerous Religion: What the Old Testament Says and Why It Matters*. Waco: Baylor University Press, 2014.

Pryor, Dwight A. *Behold the Man*. DVD series and study guide. Dayton, OH: Center for Judaic Christian Studies, 2008.

———. *Unveiling the Kingdom of Heaven*. DVD series and study guide. Dayton, OH: Center for Judaic Christian Studies, 2008.

Richards, E. Randolph and Brandon O'Brien. *Misreading Scripture with Western Eyes*. Downers Grove, IL: InterVarsity Press, 2012.

Richter, Sandra. *The Epic of Eden*. Downers Grove, IL: InterVarsity Press, 2008.

Rihbany, Abraham Mitrie. *The Syrian Christ*. New York: Houghton Mifflin, 1916.

Rudolph, David and Joe Willits, eds. *Introduction to Messianic Judaism*. Grand Rapids: Zondervan, 2013.

Safrai, Shmuel and Menahem Stern, eds. *The Jewish People in the First Century* (2 vols.). Philadelphia: Fortress Press, 1976.

Sarna, Nahum. *Understanding Genesis: The World of the Bible in Light of History*. New York: Schocken Books, 1966.

———. *Exploring Exodus: The Origins of Biblical Israel*. New York: Schocken Books, 1996.

Schechter, Solomon. *Aspects of Rabbinic Theology*. Peabody, MA: Hendrickson, 1998 (1909).

Spangler, Ann and Lois Tverberg. *Sitting at the Feet of Rabbi Jesus: How the Jewishness of Jesus Can Transform Your Faith*. Grand Rapids: Zondervan, 2009.

Stern, David H. *Jewish New Testament Commentary*. Baltimore: Messianic Jewish Resources International, 1992.

Tverberg, Lois. *Listening to the Language of the Bible: Companion Bible Study*. Holland, MI: En-Gedi Resource Center, 2005.

———. *Walking in the Dust of Rabbi Jesus: How the Jewish Words of Jesus Can Change Your Life*. Grand Rapids: Zondervan, 2012.

Tverberg, Lois with Bruce Okkema. *Listening to the Language of the Bible: Hearing It through Jesus' Ears*. Holland, MI: En-Gedi Resource Center, 2004.

Vander Laan, Ray. *Faith Lessons*. DVD series and study guides. Grand Rapids: Zondervan, 1998–2008.

Walton, John. *The Lost World of Genesis One*. Downers Grove, IL: IVP Academic, 2009.

Walton, John and Craig Keener. *Cultural Backgrounds NIV Study Bible*. Grand Rapids: Zondervan, 2016.

Wilson, Marvin. *Our Father Abraham: The Jewish Roots of the Christian Faith*. Grand Rapids: Eerdmans, 1989.

Wright, N. T. *How God Became King: The Forgotten Story of the Gospels*. New York: Harper Collins, 2012.

———. *The Challenge of Jesus: Rediscovering Who Jesus Was and Is*. Downers Grove, IL: InterVarsity Press, 1999.

Wu, Jackson. *One Gospel for all the Nations*. Pasadena, CA: William Carey Library, 2015.

Young, Brad. *Jesus the Jewish Theologian*. Peabody, MA: Hendrickson, 1995.

———. *The Parables: Jewish Tradition and Christian Interpretation*. Peabody, MA: Hendrickson, 1998.

Useful Web Resources

Our Rabbi Jesus: His Jewish Life and Teaching	OurRabbiJesus.com
En-Gedi Resource Center	EnGediResourceCenter.com
Center for Judaic-Christian Studies	JCStudies.com
That the World May Know	ThatTheWorldMayKnow.com
Jerusalem Perspective	JerusalemPerspective.com
Hebrew for Christians	Hebrew4Christians.com
Torah Class	TorahClass.com

Subject Index

Scripture Index

Lois Tverberg has been speaking and writing about the Jewish background of Christianity for the past twenty years. Her passion is to translate the Bible's ancient setting into fresh insights that deepen and strengthen Christian faith. Lois grew up with plenty of Sunday school knowledge, but it wasn't until after she had earned a PhD in biology and was teaching as a college professor that her fascination for biblical study was ignited by a seminar at her church. She has since studied several times in Israel, taking courses in biblical Hebrew, Koine Greek, and in the physical and cultural context of the Bible.

In 2001 she cofounded the En-Gedi Resource Center, an educational ministry with a goal of deepening Christian understanding of the Bible in its original context. There she published her first book, *Listening to the Language of the Bible*, a devotional guide to Hebrew words and ideas. In 2009 Lois partnered with Ann Spangler to write the bestselling *Sitting at the Feet of Rabbi Jesus*. Together they explored Jesus' Jewish reality, discovering how his Jewish context expands our understanding of his life and ministry. Later she followed up with *Walking in the Dust of Rabbi Jesus*, where she continued her journey into Jesus' world, challenging her audience to follow their Rabbi more closely by hearing his teachings in light of Jewish thought.

Lois is a Christian laywoman who brings to her writing a surprising set of tools from her training as a scientist. She received her BA in physics (1989) at Luther College in Decorah, Iowa, and her PhD in Molecular Physiology (1993) from the University of Iowa. She has published several scientific papers and holds a patent from her PhD research. For several years she taught biology at Hope College in Holland, Michigan.

Lois currently writes from her home in Holland, Michigan. She also speaks at churches, conferences, and retreats. Her current news and articles are available on her website, *Our Rabbi Jesus: His Jewish Life and Teaching*, at OurRabbiJesus.com.

Our Rabbi Jesus

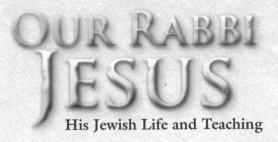

His Jewish Life and Teaching

What can we learn from Jesus' first-century world that will make his words even more powerful and life-changing?

At **OurRabbiJesus.com**, you'll find articles to reflect with me on this topic, personal updates, and resources to go deeper.

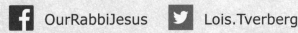

Lois Tverberg

Tverberg@OurRabbiJesus.com

OurRabbiJesus Lois.Tverberg